Sandcastles in the Tide

The Value of
Employee Communications
In the Context of Constant Change

Jack LeMenager

Address all inquiries to: Fells Publishing,
10 Johnson Road, Winchester, MA 01890

Printed in the United States of America
by CreateSpace

ISBN: 978-1497415720

Title: Sandcastles in the Tide:
The Value of Employee Communications
In the Context of Constant Change
by Jack LeMenager

1.   Employee communications
2.   Change management
3.   Employee engagement
4.   Business communications
5.   Leadership communications

Cover Design by John G. Leonard
The Granville Group
Grass Valley, CA
Cover photo: iStock.com

For Carolyn,
whose love, patience, faith and wit
have sustained me through the years.

And for Calder,
who has brought happy
rays of sunshine into our lives.

Contents

Introduction

Today, no matter what industry you're in, no matter whether yours is a private or public company, large or small, for-profit or non-profit organization, you are facing change. Change is constant. Change is today's only certainty. Change goes right down into the heart of the organization.

The ability of every employee at every level – from top to bottom – to deal with it, to adapt to it, and to take advantage of it spells the difference between organizations' success and failure.

To build an organization that's best positioned for success, leadership must develop and direct the strategy that will deal with and adapt to change, ready and able (and willing) to turn on a dime as circumstances demand. Managers need to facilitate and drive that strategy within their teams. And employees across the organization must enact it in everything they do. Getting those three components of the company in synch is the real challenge.

Unfortunately, the natural human reaction to change is resistance. It's like a child at the beach building a sandcastle. He starts modestly, abstractly. But his focus grows more intent as the castle begins to take shape.

He pours his imagination and energy into the effort, including elaborate details like towers, gatehouses, a moat and drawbridge, spires, and walls, using bits of seaside detritus to embellish the battlements.

1

As the afternoon wanes, however, his work is for naught and it's too late when he sees that the tide is rising and soon lapping at the castle's outer walls. He frantically struggles to resist the change that the incoming tide represents, digging deep diversionary canals to try to redirect the water. But it's all in vain. The tide is inevitable and will continue its inexorable rise, washing away the child's efforts.

Businesses and the individuals who comprise them can be like that child. Their sandcastles are the way they operate day-to-day. They may refine how they approach the market and customers, and they may expand their product lines, while individuals may obtain new skills of self-improvement. All the while, however, they continue operating as they always have, even as the rising tide of change begins to confront the organization, and what they do begins to lose relevance in the larger picture – until they have no choice but to do things differently or go out of business.

Change is as inevitable as the tide, and there's nothing anyone can do about it but adapt, prepare for it, be ready to operate differently, and try to make the best of a constantly evolving world, looking for new opportunities embedded in the challenges.

That's what this book is about: the inevitability of change and how we as individuals and organizations can deal with it. But it's also about the central role that employee engagement and effective internal communications can play in improving an organization's ability to adapt to and take advantage of change.

This book is a collection of essays – many of which appeared in my "Inside the Organization" blog over the past four years. Each is complete in itself and can be read independently of the others, but I have also tried to fit them together in a cohesive, progressive pattern so that they can be read consecutively from beginning to end. In that regard, I've adapted, updated, expanded, refined, and then organized them to address these key points and related issues:

- What drives change, and why it's inevitable.
- Change's multiple impacts on organizations.
- How people operate within organizations, and why they need to adapt to deal with change, and how.
- The role that employee engagement and effective internal communications play in making organizations stronger, and more nimble and responsive.
- The central position that customers must play in the equation if organizations are to succeed, and how that links back to change and effective communications.

In sum, the ultimate success of any organization in the face of constant change lies in its ability to cultivate, encourage and elicit from its people their best talents and creativity, their passion, and an eagerness to apply themselves toward helping achieve their and the organization's common mission. Employee engagement and effective communications, in their many forms, are integral to achieving those ends.

Note to second edition: This updated edition of the book, which was originally published in March 2014, includes three new essays that continue and expand on the original themes of the first edition. I hope you enjoy the book and get a lot out of it.

July 2015

I. Managing Change

I. Managing Change

"You can't control the wind, but you can adjust your sails."

Albert Einstein

Change May Be Tough, But It's What We Want

We take comfort in the routines of our lives. But change brings us ambiguity and challenges. It disrupts our habits. It forces us to rethink our mode of operating and to do something different that's often unfamiliar, perhaps even uncomfortable and difficult.

So we don't like change. Our natural reaction is to fight it. But while we may try to resist change and bristle at and carp about the stress it gives us, we are, ironically, its primary drivers.

Consider the devices we use and the services we've come to expect. Were those available to us some five, ten or fifteen years ago? Most likely, many were not. Imagine a world today without smartphones and the conveniences they give us. What about 24/7 online shopping, or the ability to watch TV programs whenever we want?

In the 1987 movie "Wall Street," many of us saw our first cell phone in the hands of the fictional Gordon Gekko. That's because this corporate raider was rich enough to afford one, which then cost thousands of dollars. By the way, the reception wasn't that great, it was about the size of a large shoe, and it weighed a couple of pounds. It may have been portable, but it wasn't very convenient.

So what happened? How did that cell phone become the slim, infinitely more versatile device in our pocket? It was consumer demand – ours – that drove the advancement of technologies and capabilities we now take for granted: the smartphone in the pocket, the HDTV in the den, and the hybrid car in the driveway.

No, we never explicitly asked for the many modern devices and conveniences we now take for granted. We never demanded that Apple create remarkable iPhone apps that allow us to accomplish a range of tasks that were never before possible.

It was incremental. Their development and evolution were driven by our unceasing and insatiable desire for *smaller, faster, higher quality, cheaper, more convenient,* and *easier.* These are the components of change.

Consumer choices become expectations.

Then expectations become demands.

Consumers' expanding choices impact you, no matter your profession. By the way, these are *your* demands and expectations. These are *my* demands and expectations.

On Monday morning, we go back to work to face the unrelenting pace of change. What passed for quality work a few years ago is unacceptable today. It's practically a firing offense.

As soon as we settle into "normative" behaviors and attitudes as deliverers of services and goods, along comes a competitor that does it better, faster, or cheaper. And we have to match it or beat it, or else we and our company will be left behind.

Our boss' demands grow greater and more overwhelming than ever before and the time we spend at work expands to meet those demands. But then, he's getting the same demands from his boss, as well as the CEO's demands, and the demands of shareholders for ever greater returns on investment. And those growing returns come from you and your team's ability to create and deliver better products and services – quicker and with higher profit margins, by the way.

It's not just our everyday devices like smartphones, TVs and the Internet. It's health care, transportation and every other component of modern life. Consider just health care, for one. We've seen such amazing advances in our lifetimes. Diseases of our youth or our parents' youth have been either eradicated or controlled, allowing continued life for many people who before would have been condemned to an early death or serious impairment.

The healthcare field – medical education, pharmaceuticals, medical devices, and delivery – continues to improve, continues to impact our lives in ever more impressive and heretofore untold ways. Again, those advances are only possible because of people's ability to adapt to and leverage change. But we have so much further to go, so many horrible diseases to conquer. And that means change and more change.

We build our societal growth and advances incrementally on what went before. That is the essence of continuous change: constant improvement on what we now have. We learn how to do it better, faster and cheaper, and we apply those lessons.

You'd better get used to it. It's a never-ending cycle. It's only going to come at us faster. Then again, we could revert to that shoe-sized cell phone. But I doubt we will.

Changing Perceptions of Change

The perceptions of change and the range of reactions to it that occur within today's businesses are as varied as the businesses themselves – and rightly so, because organizations are all unique, with their own ingrained cultural attributes and histories.

Every organization has gone through trials and triumphs, and each such experience brings with it lessons that become part of their story and institutional memory. These ultimately shape companies' attitude and approach toward their futures. It is that which guides them forward in how they deal with change.

So it's no surprise to see how two very different companies react today to multiple changes occurring in the external worlds in which they operate. These two companies are as different as night and day.

First is a large multi-division manufacturing company with deeply held traditions. The CEO worked his way up the leadership ladder, as had his predecessors. The CEO and his leadership team are accustomed to defining the current reality and directing how their managers and employees should respond.

To date, the company has seen steady growth throughout its life. But it is beginning to experience a downturn in that pattern due to a range of external factors beyond its control. Fortunately, the leadership recognizes and acknowledges those forces.

Our second example, Company Two, is a professional services company that went through agonizing trials through the economy of 2008-onwards that resulted in many of its competitors going under or merging, and many others emerging far different than they were going in. Company Two falls into this latter category: a different company today than it was in 2007.

So how are these two very different organizations dealing with change today?

The traditional command-and-control company is struggling. People are waiting for the CEO to tell them what to do. And so far, he's only told them to become empowered and start taking risks. But this runs against what they've actually seen and experienced. So people are cautiously hanging back, watching and waiting.

Company Two, on the other hand, rightly acknowledges that change is already happening to them. The leaders at Company Two speak of what they must become. But they do so in the present tense. Its leadership sees change as something that they must be doing *now*. In other words, they cannot afford merely to *plan for change*. They must *live the change constantly* – right now.

Done right, this far more aggressive approach to change becomes engrained in a company's new culture. But this is a remarkably different approach to how most companies deal with change today.

Conventionally, in the context of the business, most people think of change they will undertake at a particular point in time. They say that change is imposing itself on them and they must figure out how to respond.

It is something they will do at some point in the future, as though planning to pivot before heading off in a different direction. On the other hand, as we've grown accustomed to this notion of change as a constant state of affairs, we have come to realize that we must continuously prepare for the change that will always come at us. This is a foreign concept for most organizations. It is also almost as foreign as trying to conceive of time as the fourth dimension. Not only must we be prepared for change. We must assume that it is already happening to us and so we must become what we must be tomorrow right now.

That said, what would the world look like to Company One after it has planned and fully executed its internal changes? Likely, that external world will have further evolved, necessitating further changes.

Perhaps this is what Company Two discovered in the midst of the turmoil of the economic crisis of 2008: that change must become a permanent mindset and way of operating.

What are You Doing Today
to Reinvent Your Business for Tomorrow?

The day Apple introduced the iPod was the day it ceased being a computer company – not that many people realized that at the time. In fact, CEO Steve Jobs and chief designer Jony Ive may have been the only ones who did. But over the next few years, as succeeding and improved iterations of the pocket music player came out, the idea gradually sunk in that Apple had expanded beyond the realm of the Macintosh.

The notion became permanently etched into the public's consciousness with the subsequent introductions of the iPhone and iPad. Sure, Apple continued to produce evermore powerful, functional, and sophisticated computers and laptops. But Apple had morphed into a lifestyle company: a purveyor of tools and technologies that make our lives more pleasant, to some degree easier and, in many ways, more portable.

What Apple and Steve Jobs figured out was how those tools and technologies perfectly linked to one another to create a unified whole that redefined for the world what Apple was and what it was capable of doing and giving us.

In a similar vein, it's unlikely that anyone who draws a paycheck from Nike thinks of the company as just a maker of running shoes. When Bill Bowerman, the exceptional University of Oregon track coach, borrowed his wife's waffle iron in the 1960s to make the sole for his ideal running shoe, he launched Nike. Little about the company today would be familiar to him. His vision then was all about helping his middle-distance runners improve their performances. He didn't think about golfing equipment, basketball, baseball, or the many other sports of which Nike is now an integral part.

Today, for instance, the company's Nike+ system allows runners to monitor and track each workout by means of sensors in their shoes to download data through Bluetooth into devices like iPhones. Via the Nike+ Internet platform, runners can share performance data online and receive customized advice from Nike coaches. In his day, Bowerman used a simple analogue pocket stopwatch to check his runners' accomplishments from one meet to the next, from one practice to another. The Nike+ system is something he would have loved. But that's only one small part of what Nike does and is capable of today.

Amazon is not just an online bookseller. In addition to selling just about any and all consumer products, Amazon is now in direct competition to Netflix, streaming its own movie and TV series catalogues. Another huge and largely unknown part of its business is Amazon Web Services, a collection of remote computing services that together make up a cloud computing platform, which is, for instance, where Apple's iCloud resides.

Jeff Bezos, Amazon's founder and CEO, bought the *Washington Post* in 2013. What has that meant for Amazon (and the *Post*)? Amazon also is a book publisher, through its CreateSpace subsidiary, competing effectively against the long-established publishing houses. (By the way, this book and my previous book were both published by CreateSpace.)

Google is not just a search engine but... Well, Google is now into nearly everything: from tablets, smartphones and the Android operating system that runs them, to mapping systems, office productivity software and advertising, to (coming next) systems that enable cars to drive themselves, as well as the cars themselves.

What these companies have in common is that they didn't stand still within the narrow confines of how the world perceived and defined them. Instead, they grasped the essence of their craft, their passions, and their people's talents. They fully understood and appreciated where they excelled. They then asked themselves what all that implied, where it might take them, what was possible, and what additional resources they needed to make it happen. And they haven't stopped asking those questions yet.

Companies too numerous to name stayed affixed to the tight concept of themselves, and continued to practice their trade ever more efficiently, and repeatedly. As a result, many of them either no longer exist or are a mere shadow of their former selves: Blockbuster, Radio Shack, Borders, et al.

While being in business in a capitalist system means you must grow, growth for its own sake is ultimately fruitless. What gets people out of bed in the morning and commuting to jobs at places like Apple, Amazon, Google, and Nike is the thrill of constantly reinventing and redefining their businesses, of expanding the realm of the possible.

The growth, success and profitability that those companies subsequently realize are the *outcomes* of that effort, not the *reasons* for the pursuit. When business leaders confuse the two, the end is in sight.

What are you doing today to reinvent your business for tomorrow?

When Brands Lose Their Way

All too often, iconic brands lose their way. Polaroid. PanAm. Wang. Digital Equipment (DEC). The history of business is littered with such stories. But why did these once industry-leading companies stumble? They were pioneers in their fields. Yet, these brand names are no longer with us.

Collapses like those occur for a variety of reasons, depending on the circumstances. They can arise from a combination of factors, such as when the economic climate creates conditions and opportunities for an upstart competitor to poach customers with a less-expensive alternative and/or a more robust version of the industry leader's standard model.

Like change itself, the failure is gradual and incremental. It happens because the industry leader is slow to respond to an evolving marketplace, placing false confidence in an established position atop the market. Perhaps it's just hubris.

Polaroid – and Kodak, for that matter – both reacted too slowly or too late to the advent and quick adoption of digital photography. PanAm didn't adapt to a newly competitive airline industry when regulatory controls were eased, opening the field to a plethora of discount competitors. Likewise, Wang and DEC ignored the coming of the PC, first from IBM and then the so-called clones. Where are Wang and Digital today? Wang, the first maker of office space word processors, struggled to survive in the face of the onslaught of far more versatile less costly personal computers. Failing to expand its machines' capabilities to compete effectively against the plethora of PCs flooding the market, Wang eventually declared bankruptcy.

About 1990, when his company led its industry, Digital's founding CEO, Ken Olsen, disdained PCs, saying, "The personal computer will fall flat on its face in business." He regarded them as "toys" used for "playing video games." DEC was sold off piecemeal to other companies in the late 1990s.

At the heart of such failures, we can usually find a lazy certitude – dare I say an arrogance – that the *status quo* will continue *ad infinitum*. That belief is accompanied by a loss of connection between the people who comprise the companies and the essence of their brand – i.e., what it stands for. Brands must stand for promises made to customers – be it quality, cutting edge technology, responsiveness, superior customer service, or any number of other reasons or combination of reasons for people to choose one brand over the competition.

Companies stumble because the brand promise gradually erodes and becomes empty bravado, echoing an earlier self-image built on promises that were actually delivered. This bluster masks a reality of unfulfilled promises and a lack of requisite confidence of the people that make brands live every day.

This confidence is built on leaders, managers and employees living the brand promise every day in every thing they do. But when companies lose that confidence, that connection to what the brand once stood for, it spreads across the organization – and it festers.

Lack of confidence produces more of the same and greater disassociation from the promise of meeting or exceeding customer expectations, and it permeates the customer experience. This can be a natural trend in any business, but now, the speed at which change can unfold and impact organizations is much faster than ever before.

Spotting such trends and arresting them begins by recognizing and acknowledging that the organization has lost its way, lost its core meaning, lost touch with what made it great and the leader in its field in the first place. It may still be the industry leader, but it won't be much longer if its promise is being eroded by an organization-wide disconnect.

It is coasting on its established reputation. It is moving from one quarter to the next focused on revenue and profitability, but without a shared sense of purpose or definition of what it is, or what it stands for. Is this your company today?

What are your brand promise, vision, and mission? Are they just words on paper, or are the employees, managers and leaders really living them in what they do every day? Are the words and phrases dynamic? Do they evolve as circumstances change, or are they a mere snapshot of what your company was once upon a time?

The challenge around reviving a brand or market position is not so much a revision or reiteration of the words and phrases that describe the brand. Rather, it is reconnecting every person in the organization and what they do to the true meaning of the venture – its core purpose, mission, vision, and the promises it makes to its stakeholders. The outcome of that exercise may very well be a complete revision of the brand promise, mission and vision.

But at the outset, put aside completely any temptation to fixate on words and images. Rather, work to guide individual employees to rediscover and rebuild their confidence in what the company and the brand signify, thereby reaffirming the brand promise. Assure their focus is on continuing to deliver on the promise that the brand represents so that customer experiences reaffirm it.

The Impermanence of Corporate Culture

About 2006, a friend of mine – I'll call him "Bob" – joined a Silicon Valley start-up, which I will call "Dot.Com." He was among the first employees and knew he was taking a career risk. But at the time, he was young, single, and feeling the urge to pursue new challenges and new experiences in a new place.

More than eight years later, he was one of the veterans. In the office, he often wore a San Francisco Giants jersey with the number "12" because he is Employee #12 – that is, the twelfth person to join the company that now numbers well over two-thousand people in locations around the world.

When it came time for his company to go public, he stood to reap an immense financial windfall from his tens of thousands of stock options. Yet, at the same time, he was eager to leave.

When I asked why, Bob replied that the company isn't the same as it was in its founding days. He explained that the sense of camaraderie that had infused and inspired the core team as it worked long hours and struggled to launch its web-based services model has evaporated. In its place are policies, procedures, politics, and hassles – and not as much fun, either, he added.

I pressed the question, wondering whether the culture of the organization had changed. How exactly has Dot.Com changed, I asked him? "We worked hard. We worked long hours, and we played hard. We all pitched in to get the job done. We had a strong sense of what we were going to accomplish, and why. We had a great idea and felt we would conquer the world with it. We went about it in a totally focused way, as a team."

"So what's changed," I asked? "Why do you want to leave now just as the company goes public?"

"Look," he replied, "we still work hard. But it feels like a different company now, with a different sense of mission. It's seems like we're only chasing the buck now," he said, "instead of the excitement of the new."

That Bob is leaving is not an uncommon phenomenon in that world. Previously successful start-ups like Apple, Microsoft, Google, Twitter, Facebook, and countless others experienced mass migrations within months of their IPOs. Newly wealthy, a lot of their leading talent felt liberated and cut the strings, desirous of riding that adrenaline rush of a roller coaster again. So there's that aspect to consider, too – that desire to experience the thrill of newness and creation all over again.

But the transience that is a corporate culture intrigues me and invites further exploration. How does a company culture form? What sustains it? Is culture permanent? Does a company culture evolve with time? How? Why? What was Dot.Com's culture, versus what it is now?

The short answer is, a culture is no more static and definable than is the business organization in which it lives. We know from experience and observation that static businesses ultimately cease being.

In that change and challenges will always assault organizations, remaining a stubbornly unchanging operation is a recipe for eventual failure. So the culture of the organization evolves with the changes, challenges and opportunities that the business confronts and surmounts. It helps to read what an academic has to say on the subject. MIT's Edgar Schein, one of foremost scholars on culture, says...

> *"Organizational culture is a pattern of basic assumptions – invented, discovered or developed by a given group as it learns to cope with its problems of external adaptation and internal integration – that has worked well enough to be considered valid and, therefore, to be taught to new members as the correct way to perceive, think, and feel in relation to those problems."*

Okay, that's a long-winded (but accurate) way to describe the internal dynamic of a team as its members confront the issues and tests that comprise the foundation of an enterprise's creation. As Schein goes on to point out, the culture of an organization evolves – in fact, it must evolve – to adapt to the evolution of the world in which it operates. Again, as noted here (and more famously by Charles Darwin), a failure to adapt is to accept expiration.

So if we think about the many external inputs that impose change on organizations, it's obvious why a culture evolves. As Bob's company grew, its opportunities expanded. The size, sophistication and demands of its growing customer base grew too. What satisfied Dot.Com's early customers – many of which were also small businesses – wouldn't work for the far more demanding and exacting Fortune 100 companies it was now servicing.

Dot.Com hired additional staff to help solve the fresh unknowns, problems and challenges its newer customers brought it. And with each new staff member came a new way of approaching such challenges. Those new approaches may or may not have meshed well with the culture of the previously small company.

With each new challenge and with each new staffer, the

culture changed just a little. Amassed over the eight years of an improving balance sheet, with dozens and then hundreds of new employees being added, the culture originally known and embraced by Bob and his teammates from the early days had evaporated. That sense of fellowship in confronting and conquering the early challenges was gone.

Is that a good thing? Well, if Dot.Com is a thriving business, solving heretofore-unsolvable problems for other businesses, then yes, it's a good thing. But if you're Bob, longing for the exciting days of being part of a startup, it probably isn't. No wonder it's time for Bob to move on.

Change is a good thing because with it can come growth, success and profitability. And an evolving culture.

Can Corporate Culture be Measured?

In the course of our work, the phrase "corporate culture" occurs frequently. Maybe an executive says his company's culture is "dysfunctional." Another executive may say his company has a strong "ethical culture," or another has an "inclusive culture."

But that begs the question. What exactly does "culture" mean in the context of a business organization? Briefly, an organizational culture is invented, discovered or developed over time by a given group of people (usually its founders and/or leaders) as it adjusts to and copes with its many external challenges until an acceptable pattern of behavior is established.

Those behaviors are then reinforced with employees, and introduced formally to new employees during onboarding. The culture of a company often comes alive in its vision, mission and values, particularly when that organization stays closely aligned with them, encouraging the behaviors that reinforce them.

In actual practice, a culture defines the organization and how it responds to the competitive marketplace. That said, is a company's "culture" quantifiable? Is it possible to measure it, and then to determine whether the culture within any given organization is good or bad? For instance, is the culture currently bad but moving in the right direction toward becoming good – or vice-versa?

Apparently so, if the words of New York Fed President William Dudley are to be taken seriously. The *Wall Street Journal* reported in a Feb. 2, 2015, front-page story that he is considering means of measuring banks' culture to determine whether they are "ethical" organizations, in addition to the Fed's usual checks of their overall health and fitness to stay in business.

The article alludes to the application of such measures as a prelude to justifying a bank's break-up into smaller entities – which presupposes that smaller financial institutions are more likely to operate ethically and within the law than larger ones.

Similarly, the U.S. Comptroller of the Currency Thomas Curry was also quoted in the same article saying that culture is a "critical component of a sound management team" – which is tantamount to saying that a car needs four tires to move, though not whether those tires are bald or flat and therefore dangerous.

Coming off the 2008-2009 collapse and near-collapse of a number of American financial institutions, Congress and the government's various agencies have been working towards tightening existing and developing new regulatory controls to minimize the likelihood of such breakdowns in the future. So Mr. Dudley believes that one approach in achieving that may lie in measuring and, by implication, regulating an organization's culture.

The article further notes that banks already are reactively trying to do just that, collectively spending tens of millions of dollars on outside consultants who are only too happy to take their money. The measurements undertaken so far seem mostly to involve employee satisfaction surveys, based on the supposition that satisfied employees are more likely to be ethical in their business practices.

It would be rash were government regulators to impose such tests and standards as pre-conditions for certifying and recertifying financial institutions. The initial effect would be chaos and fear. The long-term result would be closely attuned behaviors to match what the banks believe regulators are looking for. Meanwhile, the root problem in terms of ethical versus unethical behaviors will remain unaddressed. And we will, no doubt, continue to see the "perp walks" of indicted senior Wall Street executives.

To expand on Mr. Curry's self-obvious statement, a principled company leadership team builds an ethical culture in at least two ways: by the examples it sets for the organization, and through its management practices, policies and procedures.

A CEO, for instance, who professes ethical behavior to subordinates and the public, but does the opposite in actual practice is not setting a good example of ethical behavior. Conversely, open dialogue and honesty within the company's top tiers will translate into those same behaviors down through the organization's managers and supervisors, particularly when those positive and appropriate actions are reinforced with reward and recognition – or, conversely, with reprimands or dismissals when those actions are inappropriate.

Similarly, the right behaviors in an ethical culture are also underpinned by a cogent vision/mission/values statement, and established (and enforced) policies and procedures driven across the organization and from top to bottom. That means behaviors that adhere to appropriate business practices, thereby staying within the bounds of legal operations in the eyes of regulators like the Fed.

But back to William Dudley's contention in the *Journal* article... The fact is, corporate culture is amorphous and not readily quantifiable. Culture, whether a national culture or that of an institution, is like the human personality. You may describe someone's personality by using words like "friendly," "engaging," "serious" – or their opposites. You may judge that Person A is friendlier or more serious than Person B, but that kind of judgment is purely subjective. It does not mean you can measure the difference in any quantifiable way. The same is true with organizational culture.

Navigating By Your Own North Star

Leaders know the critical importance of a vision to guide them and their company around the shoals of constant change to achieve success. They expend enormous resources developing and acting on that vision within their management teams to drive their organization forward, through the uncertainties that change imposes.

The most successful leaders are also adept at sharing, communicating, and constantly nurturing that vision with their employees, ensuring that the entire company is focused on the same ideal, navigating always toward the same destination – in the direction of their "North Star," if you will.

An insightful blog entry in early 2012, "What Wise Leaders Always Follow," posted on the HBR Insight Center (*Harvard Business Review*), provided practicable guidance to business leaders in identifying their own North Star and how to follow it. Author Prasad Kaipa, a senior fellow in the Center for Leadership, Innovation and Change at the Indian School of Business (Hyderabad, India), argued that wise leaders "root themselves in a noble purpose, align it with a compelling vision, and then take action... That noble purpose becomes a *North Star*, giving direction when the path ahead is hazy, humility when arrogance announces false victory, and inspiration when the outlook seems bleak."

Indeed, as Kaipa points out, "Though it is not always simple to find one's North Star, once it appears, its guidance helps simplify one's choices... It becomes their calling, and they service that calling willingly, happily, and infectiously." The key word in that quote is "infectiously" because, in order to be compelling, a North Star must be infectious in its conciseness, while the leader that communicates it must endow it with real world meaning, enthusiasm, and passion.

Employees and line managers readily sense their leaders' zeal. It spreads in the same way that a political cause can suddenly catch fire when a politician succinctly verbalizes a guiding principle that people immediately understand, identify with, and latch onto.

Pres. John Kennedy's admonition that "we choose to go to the moon" conveyed a common desire and, ultimately, a destiny. He gave the nation an ideal to aim for, something that the people could visualize and strive for. Everyone directly and indirectly involved in the space program instinctively sensed his or her role in reaching for Kennedy's North Star – a destiny that, in fact, out-lived Kennedy. The nation rose to the challenge and succeeded. The citizenry was universally enthusiastic and supportive – despite the decade's turmoil of Vietnam, assassinations and race riots.

Kaipa illustrates his essay by discussing at length the Aravind Eye Care System and the North Star that its founder, Dr. Govindappa Venkataswammy fixed on to start the company: "To eliminate needless blindness by providing appropriate, compassionate, high-quality eye care for all." Kaipa says it was a "seemingly impossible dream." To support it, the founder developed a simple set of principles: Turn no one away regardless of ability to pay; give everyone the same high quality care; and don't be dependent on outside funding sources.

Though he doesn't say it outright, we can infer that Dr. Venkataswammy's North Star and guiding principles inspired not only his employees, but also everyone it touched. There's something powerful and empowering about being associated with a cause whose North Star is like that. Your North Star needn't be so lofty or altruistic, but it should match your desires, affinities, abilities, and reach, especially those of your employees.

A compelling North Star and its infectiousness can also serve as an effective recruiting tool, attracting exactly the kinds of people who are inspired by it and thus eager to apply their skills and energies to help the organization attain it. Equally important, it attracts customers and builds brand loyalty.

Communicating your North Star becomes an all-encompassing affair, reaching not just the internal audience but also customers, venders, and investors. People feel more connected to a business when they sense its guiding spirit and want to invest in it themselves, either by buying its products or stocks, or joining the effort as an employee.

Perhaps Apple is the best contemporary example of a company that has identified its North Star and effectively communicated it to its internal and external audiences. Steve Jobs famously said he wanted to "put a dent in the universe" – a new age way of saying that he wanted Apple truly to change the way people lived their lives.

Apple became successful because it –especially, Steve Jobs – created and effectively communicated its North Star. More important, Apple established a pattern of breakthrough products and services that repeatedly validated its North Star. Each time it did so, it reinforced its core principles while increasing employee and customer loyalty – which is about as good it gets for a business organization.

Living on Technology's Leading Edge

Toward the end of the nineteenth century and in early years of the twentieth, one of the biggest problems confronting the people of New York City was the massive volume of horse manure in the streets. In addition to its offensive odor and having to step carefully when crossing a street, there was a constant health hazard, especially in the hot summer months.

The city's leaders wrestled with means to control it. Increasing the numbers of cleaning crews wasn't enough. Among the proposals considered was putting limits on the number of horses allowed in the city. But that wasn't practical. America's most populous city, like all others, relied on horses to pull the carriages that conveyed passengers, and the wagons that delivered essential goods.

About the time the city fathers were at wit's end, their problem began to go away in a totally unexpected way: The arrival of the internal combustion engine and the growing acceptance of the mass-produced automobile. Within a decade or two, nearly all horses – and horse manure – disappeared from the streets of New York, replaced by horseless carriages. Problem solved.

In a similar vein, in the last decade of the twentieth century, owners of office buildings scrambled to retrofit their structures with miles and miles of Ethernet cable to accommodate the need to connect all desktop computers to the Internet and local area networks. Yet, despite the massive investments in money and man-hours, within a decade, the need for Ethernet was virtually eliminated with the advent and widespread adoption of WiFi.

Both these circumstances point up a core irony of technology: While we all welcome the capabilities and conveniences that technology gives us, at the same time it is not something that we can foresee and easily anticipate. Rather, it is something for which it is nearly impossible to plan.

Consequently, no matter how prescient we may think we are as a society, it is impossible to foresee the effects that an unimagined technology would have on our lives and our infrastructure.

This challenge occurred to me while taking a tour of my town's aging high school, which was badly in need of replacement. Over the years, the school administration had cobbled together various upgrades to sustain a campus that would provide the most current, safest learning environment. But eventually, they just ran out of options.

Take yourself back to the late 1960s when the school was being designed and built. Try to imagine what a high school building would require in terms of infrastructure fifty years hence. For one, they would need a library with enough shelf space to accommodate thousands and thousands of books, including encyclopedia sets.

So here we were, fifty years later, and it was time to replace that dinosaur whose the library has been renamed the "Media Center," with a fraction of the numbers of books envisioned when it was designed and built. In their places are computer workstations, which no one could have imagined fifty years ago, a Wikipedia that has made all those sets of encyclopedia obsolete.

This dinosaur of a high school also has miles of unused Ethernet cable that had been strung above classroom ceiling panels some twenty years before, and a computer center located in the same classroom where many high school girls (and yes, it was mostly girls) thirty or forty years before had learned to type on new electric typewriters in anticipation of joining the secretarial pool after graduation.

And that's to say nothing of the changes and accompanying expenses that new regulations and laws would impose on public buildings – including schools – the most demanding of which was the Americans with Disabilities Act of 1990. In addition, the advances in energy efficient construction alone make replacement imperative, if for no other reason than to save gobs of money in fuel and electricity costs.

How do we account for changes that we cannot comprehend needing forty, fifty or even sixty years from now? If we couldn't anticipate WiFi less than ten years before it became widespread, how are we going to anticipate the next unknown technological leap and accommodate it accordingly? Thinking about business, how can we anticipate and incorporate the necessary changes that we cannot know?

The short answer is, we can't. But, we must approach such unknowns with an open, inquiring mind, recognizing that today's decisions work best in today's world, and that we shouldn't get too invested in them, anticipating that they will likely lose their relevance. In thinking through those decisions, in weighing the pros and cons of one choice versus another, are we adequately considering unknowns?

Those "what if's" can come back to haunt us. Those decisions that involve multimillion-dollar capital investments must be made in the context of a discrete timeframe, fully cognizant that even that could shift quickly if something as momentous as the invention of the mass assembled automobile comes along to wipe the slate clean. Our planning window of opportunity, by the way, shrinks as fast as technology advances. A ten-year planning time frame is a vanishing luxury – if it exists at all.

At its core, that's what change is all about. That's what we need to manage for, no matter the nature of our business. It means we must be nimble, always open to new ideas and new ways of thinking about challenges and potential solutions and opportunities. We can't afford to be arrogant in believing that today's planning will see us through the coming decades without tweaks and course corrections along the way.

Admonishing for Greatness

"Success breeds complacency. Complacency breeds failure. Only the paranoid survive."

Andy Grove, former Intel CEO

Attending my client company's quarterly internal town hall, I watched as the CEO stood before the gathered employees, both those present in the room as well as those watching the live webcast around the country. After announcing record earnings and profits for the third quarter, he read glowing analysts' reports and congratulated the employees on their hard work.

And then, practically in the same breath, he said, "Now, get over it. That's behind us. Time to get back to work." Pausing for effect, he looked around the room and spoke firmly, "Two or three years from now, let us not look back on this quarter and say that it was the best we'd ever done. Because I know we can do better."

Was it a classic example of the *"What have you done for me lately?"* syndrome? Perhaps yes, at least in part. But at the same time, at the heart of such a leadership admonition is a firm belief in the organization's ability to excel, to do better today than yesterday, to continue innovating, and to create and pursue new opportunities while dealing with unrelenting change and fending off competitive challenges.

Indeed, it is leadership's job to steel employees' courage, to reinforce their determination to excel, and to bolster their confidence, all the while encouraging their commitment to and faith in the company's mission – which the CEO did as he continued to talk.

His speech and his answers to subsequent employee questions in the town hall meeting were emblematic of the driving force behind the company's continuing success, and its ability to impress both Wall Street analysts and its customers.

In fact, as the CEO ran down the numbers, he cited an unacceptable level of customer attrition. "Yes, it's true" he admitted. "We're not as bad as our competitors. We're not losing customers as quickly as they are. But our trend line is going in the wrong direction and we need to address that immediately. What are we doing that is driving our customers away? We need to find out and address that directly and firmly."

Through the course of the one-hour session, he and his executive team did exactly that. They talked about the company's weaknesses that likely were the cause of customers' lost loyalty. Their talks and the way they shared data included a broad brush stroke of responsibility on everyone in the organization, not just those with customer-facing roles, but those who support them and those who develop and produce the products and services that attract new customers and keep them coming back. This is one formula for success, for assuring a controlled, intelligent evolution of the company.

To illustrate his point about the need for continuing innovation and creativity, the CEO gave a quick review of the organization's recent history, which revealed that in the previous fiscal year, its top sources of revenue and profit had come from products and services that it hadn't even been offering as recently as five years earlier. He noted that those new products and services came from research, development and invention, or through acquisition of companies with complementary product and service lines.

In the context of momentous change, to survive, grow and thrive from one quarter to the next, from one fiscal year to the next, the company and its leadership focused on reinvesting, reinventing and always thinking about and always trying to see the company in a different light. What defined the company in 2005, the CEO noted, would barely be recognizable in 2015.

When a corporate leader like this CEO cajoles and admonishes the troops to raise the bar, to top last quarter's numbers, that is a live, real-time enactment of the very real impact of constant change on an organization, providing guidance and encouragement toward the paths that will sustain and grow the business through the present and future uncertainties.

Many once-great brand names are no longer with us, as noted in "When Brands Lose Their Way" (page 15). Wang, PanAm, Polaroid, Blockbuster and now, it seems, BlackBerry: once-great brand names, now fading or gone, remaining only in our memories. Of course, with BlackBerry, the devices will linger for a few years as users gradually upgrade their smartphones to other models, devices either from Samsung, Apple, Nokia or some other manufacturer.

From a leadership perspective, what's the difference between these faded and lost brand names and a company like my client? It's a constant vigilance – modeled by the CEO and the leadership team – always on the lookout for ways to be better, for avenues to overcome or sidestep challenges. But it's also being on your toes, expecting and anticipating unknown challenges from people, places and organizations that may be unimaginable today.

That's what Andy Grove meant when he said, "Only the paranoid survive."

The Leadership Lessons of George Washington

Given the choice between working for a manager who operates in a top-down fashion issuing orders without benefit of alternative opinions, versus one who seeks a diversity of input, most of us would prefer to work for the latter. I dare say, too, that the latter type is more likely to be successful in the long run, by a number of measures.

Most of us would presume that George Washington was a successful leader. But do we know why?

There are few historic leaders that garner as much praise as George Washington. The "Father of our Country" is credited with winning the American War for Independence, as well as providing the right vision at the right time to help guide the establishment of our Constitution, and serving as our first President, setting the standard and precedents for all those that followed.

But it was a book, "Washington's Crossing," by David Hackett Fischer, that really opened my eyes to the man's truly distinctive leadership qualities. In school, we learned the abbreviated and hackneyed story of Washington – the cherry tree fable and all that mythology.

I don't recall delving into the specifics of his character, what made him a great leader. Fischer's book covers a brief chunk of the history of the Revolutionary War, from December 1776 to the following spring, but therein digs into Washington's uniquely supreme character. In those four to five months, the Continental

Army, under the astute and wise leadership of Washington, reversed the fortunes of the Continentals and changed the course of the war. By comparing the leadership style of Washington to that of his British counterparts, Gen. Sir William Howe and, more specifically, Gen. Charles Cornwallis, Fischer demonstrates why Washington really was a great leader.

A key characteristic of our first President, as revealed in this portrayal, was his unique ability to respond to rapidly changing circumstances, to think clearly and strategically while soliciting a diversity of ideas and opinions from his team.

To recap the story, the British army had chased the Americans out of Long Island and Manhattan, into and across New Jersey in the last weeks of 1776. The rebels' fortunes looked dismal as they crossed the Delaware River and made winter camp in Pennsylvania.

As the year approached its end, the British and their Hessian allies prepared to continue their march into Pennsylvania with the goal of overwhelming and occupying Philadelphia, the Continentals' capital. But with a bold and highly risky strategy, Washington took the offensive, leading his ragtag army back across the ice-choked Delaware on Christmas night, surprising and overwhelming the Hessian camp in Trenton the following morning.

Two days later, they fended off the reinforcing Redcoats and again went on the offensive by attacking the British stronghold at Princeton. The two successive victories turned the tide of the war in at least three important ways.

First, they provided both the Continental army and the Continental Congress with their first major successes of the war and an important boost in confidence. Second, that confidence bump helped recruit badly needed fresh troops while drawing equally critical supplies from reluctant backers. Third, British and Hessian armies' losses badly shook their confidence, from the officer corps to the rank and file, and put them off-balance and on the defensive. Americans' victories also put them on the offense, where they would remain for the balance of the war.

By the spring of 1777, opposition leaders in Parliament in London began arguing that it was time to pull out of the conflict, Parliament being reluctant to grant Howe's desperate requests for supplemental troops and supplies.

Through the winter and early spring months of 1777, Americans continually harassed the opposition in the so-called "forage wars" of New Jersey, preventing the British and Hessians from obtaining critical feed for their horses and thereby reducing their mobility – the equivalent of denying gasoline and diesel supplies to a modern army.

Through it all, as the Fischer repeatedly illustrates, it was Washington's superior leadership style that made the difference. In one passage, he draws the clear distinctions between the foes:

> "...Cornwallis imposed his plan from the top down, against the judgment of able inferiors, and prepared to attack in the morning. [Meanwhile,] Washington in his council of war welcomed the judgment of others and presided over an open process of discovery and decision that yielded yet another opportunity. In the night, Washington disengaged his forces from an enemy only a few yards away, and an exhausted American army found the will and strength to make another night march toward Princeton."

You can sense the rigidly hierarchical style of the professional British general, bound up in the traditions of his army, while not brooking any alternative ideas or input from his officer corps, blindly moving ahead with his own plan. Washington came from a different stock, with a far more democratic army and officer corps. It would have been anathema of him to ignore or not seek the thoughts and ideas of his senior officers. And when he did, time and again it made the difference between victory and defeat.

The more effective American presidents over the years have been those that assume the role of the senior executive – Lincoln, Kennedy and Reagan come to mind – presidents who surrounded themselves with a diversity of viewpoints, and sought the full range of opinions and insights before reaching a conclusive and final decision. The less effective presidents have been those that wasted precious time to build and reach consensus among their advisors. Or those that led without benefit of alternative viewpoints and ideas, and micro-managed. Or those who found themselves paralyzed by tough challenges, unable to make critical decisions.

Washington's leadership style endures and remains highly applicable in a range of modern and conventional challenges, including those that occur within the world of business – i.e., managing a diverse organization in the face of constant change, change that can at times seem tantamount to going to war.

Clearly, in this way, George Washington established the model for the ideal leader, not just in the military, but also in politics and business.

Activating a Corporate Initiative

One of the most challenging tasks for any manager, often layered on top of many daily responsibilities and activities, is activating a new corporate initiative or strategy. These plans often originate at the senior-most levels of the organization and fall on the shoulders of the managers to enact, sometimes without sufficient support or forethought, unfortunately.

Most corporate initiatives begin with the best of intentions, often compelled by external changes that confront organizations with vast and complex challenges. To succeed, such initiatives ultimately require change at the individual employee level. In other words, everybody, regardless of role and responsibilities, must reinvent the way they do their job. And that means behavior and attitude change.

However, where most initiatives fall apart, as our experience has shown, is in their execution. They're well planned and launched with much fanfare and attention-getting activities. The CEO and her/his executive team are suddenly highly visible to the organization, talking and writing through various means about the need for change and what is compelling it.

Sometimes, initiatives are branded with catchy names or phrases, and banners and posters hung around the organization's facilities urging everyone to do "X" in support of the initiative. But then, things go back to the *status quo ante*, and everyone returns to doing their jobs as they always had. Banners and posters become wallpaper – scuffed, dusty, torn, and largely ignored. The individual employee looks around, sees nothing has really changed, and proceeds accordingly as she/he had done before.

Somewhere down the line, the senior team notices, for instance, that market share slippage is continuing unabated. They see the same external forces still threatening the company's viability and future. They realize that everyone has resumed their old ways of doing things. Why?

If they're honest with themselves, it's likely because they themselves were not role models of change. For instance, if the initiative included severe spending cutbacks and headcount reduction, but employees saw that senior executives still got curb-side limo service to and from work every day, the message sent to employees was that the changes being sought were not universal. The CEO and the senior team were not demonstrating the kinds of behaviors and individual sacrifice and change they expected from the rest of the organization.

The most effective change initiatives are well planned ahead of their actual rollout – planning that anticipates the natural fall-off in interest that accompanies most of these types of efforts. Messages are developed and tested. Managers and supervisors are brought into the effort early, fully informed of the rationale for the changes being sought, and provided the necessary background information and details to help them bolster the case to the larger employee audience.

Regardless of what the initiative is, how broadly it encompasses the organization, and how thorough the pre-planning and message preparation is, the first thing any manager must do is secure as much information about it as possible, review the information, and then check her/his understanding by asking the following questions:

- Does it make sense?
- Does it answer the *"why"* and *"what's in it for me"* questions that employees will ask implicitly, if not explicitly?
- Is there any missing information, background, data or context?
- What questions does the manager still have? (If managers and supervisors still have questions after a well thought out introduction, it's likely their team members will, too.)

The second step, then, is to fill those information gaps and get answers to the outstanding questions. Central to this process is the Employee Communications team, whose role is to distill the essence of the initiative into words, ideas and context that are meaningful to people, linking it clearly to the larger corporate vision and mission.

Then, Employee Communications must help guide individual unit managers to make the message germane to their teams and what each individual must do – that is, relevant to their specific function within the organization and their individual responsibilities. Only then can managers begin to prepare to present the initiative to their teams. They should proceed not in a top-down way but rather in a discussion mode, where employees have the opportunity to talk about it, ask questions and voice concerns.

Employees may not agree with the decision (initiative), but if they understand its context and rationale, they will be more likely to enact it, and more receptive to procedural changes, even if they disagree with the over-riding effort. For senior level executives and communicators intent on guiding a major change initiative through to success, it is critical to keep this localized context in mind.

At the same time, of equal importance are actions, the active, visible buy-in by the CEO and her/his senior team, modeling the behavior changes they expect from the rest of the organization – not just at launch time but as ongoing habits, central to their personal management style.

These leadership behavior changes need to be visible, substantiated by the ongoing flow of messages. Picking up on the previous example of curb-side executive car service, if the initiative involves severe cutbacks across the organization, the CEO and his/her team members should be seen driving themselves to work every day, and parking in the employee lot – and not in specially reserved "executive" spaces near the front door, by the way.

That way, the *demonstrated* change in behaviors becomes something that employees can see, can easily understand, and can relate to, helping them find it easier to buy into the initiative, too.

Logo Change Should Also Signal Internal Changes

More often than not, struggling organizations tend to resort to cosmetic or superficial moves in attempts to gain some positive momentum. Often, the results are less than satisfactory. One example from a few years ago: American Airlines.

"We thought it was time to update the look — it's been forty years," Thomas Horton, chief executive of American's parent, AMR Corp., said in an interview in early January, 2013, as he announced they'd be changing their fleet's livery (aircrafts' exterior paint job).

Horton was relatively new to the organization at the time, having assumed the CEO position the same day the company let go former CEO Gerald Arpey and filed for bankruptcy, Nov. 29, 2011.

When American's parent, AMR, filed for bankruptcy – just as the pilots' union was threatening a strike – it had $24.7 billion in assets, $29.6 billion in debt, and $4.1 billion in cash. Its stated intention in the filing was to lower labor costs.

American was also in the news in early 2013 as US Airways was seeking to merge. And amid all this turmoil and uncertainty, the big announcement from CEO Horton was that they had decided to change their planes' color scheme.

A ballpark figure on the cost of repainting a fleet the size of American's is a bit shy of $100 million. A new paint job for a Boeing 737, a typical mid-size airliner, costs about $150,000. American's fleet then numbered 608 planes of all sizes. A quick check at the airports indicates that American has finished the job. After all that, they had to deal with the 339 planes that US Airways would be bringing to the newly merged company.

Concurrent with Horton's announcement, American ran full-page four-color ads in the national editions of the Wall Street Journal (approximately $55,000) and the New York Times (approximately $24,000), bearing a soaring Boeing 777 with sparse copy in the clouds:

> *"There is a change in the air. Introducing the new look of American, inspired by the past, but driven by the future. As we continue our journey forward, we are proud to bear the name American."*

The visual image change was likely intended as a signal for new operating policies aimed at improving the customer experience, building on the history of this nearly 80-year-old carrier. But these are my assumptions. Unless you were on the inside, you couldn't know for sure what was actually going on within American Airlines as its leadership strove to get its house in order and the business back on firmer footing. Certainly they were working with creditors and the bankruptcy court to revise AMR's debt obligations, and dealing with related matters.

But my interest in this situation lies with the people side of the equation and what the livery change communicated to the employees, because that's what will ultimately determine the company's future course and success. To that point, in situations like this one, I pose a few open-ended questions:

- In what ways did CEO Horton and his team mend fences with its unions?
- What kinds of solutions did they propose so that they could move forward productively with its unions?

- How did they communicate those solutions to the unions?
- Were they listening attentively to union leadership's ideas and responding appropriately?
- Were they actively seeking to create and sustain an on-going dialogue with union leadership to achieve long-lasting labor peace?
- Did they engage their employees in the challenges and opportunities the organization faced? How?
- What did they do to create an internal environment of dialogue, a constructive atmosphere where leadership listens to and considers other ideas?

American Airlines is an organization with a long, proud history. We've seen other historical carriers go away in similar circumstances: Pan Am and Eastern, to name just two. It would be a shame if AMR executives failed to adapt to changing times with novel approaches to their bigger challenges.

But the best thing companies in similar circumstances can do going forward is to use the image change as an avenue to improve dialogue with their employees to help illustrate the very real changes that must be undertaken by everyone if the organization is to achieve a successful turnaround.

In those cases, leadership should strive to help employees gain clearer awareness and understanding of the company's challenges and opportunities, and their respective roles in addressing them. That is always going to be the key for weakened or stymied companies emerging as strong players once again.

When *"Bringing The Outside World In"* Means China

The world outside our organization's figurative four walls is in a constant state of flux. So a central component of any internal communications effort must be to bring the external realities of the world that are driving that into the internal dialogue.

One of the employee communications function's chief responsibilities must be to keep employees informed and up-to-date on the external forces that impact the organization: the real, implicit and potential threats and opportunities, and what they mean to the way the business operates now and in the near-term.

"Bringing the outside in" is a shorthand way of referencing that imperative. But these days, for an American-based company, it can mean so much more than just keeping your employees apprised of what the competition is up to, or the state of the economy and its impact on them and your company.

It can also mean helping them understand the *people* they're competing against – particularly China, which has surpassed Japan to become the world's second largest economy, second only to the United States.

American workers are paid more than Chinese workers and have a better standard of living. But do they work better, harder and smarter, too? Can Americans make better products at a comparable cost to their Chinese counterparts who are paid far less and live in less desirable circumstances? If so, how soon will it be before the Chinese surpass us in productivity, quality and sophistication?

How (and why) do we communicate those differences to our organizations and our employees? Frankly, that's a picture that has rarely been presented to most American workers. Instead, they are urged to work harder and smarter because their company is struggling to compete against cheaper Chinese imports. Or, worse, one day they learn their jobs have gone to China – or Thailand, or India, or Vietnam, or....

I once caught a snippet of a radio commentary that insisted that America's manufacturing base, while not what it once was, still leads the world in productivity and output. Assuming that's true, it's not too late to save what's left, and make it better and more competitive. I believe we can always do better, and that communications can play a big role in achieving that improvement by helping raise awareness and understanding among our employees of exactly who they and we are competing against.

American workers are not competing against some amorphous, nefarious, faceless Chinese company. They are competing against people not unlike themselves: people with families to support; people with aspirations; people able and willing to work hard; people who may have low short-term expectations, but high long-term hopes and dreams.

Let's imagine ourselves as a Chinese peasant. We're living in a modest hovel in central China, eking out a living. The government announces it is going to build a new factory in the nearby village. Very soon, thousands of new jobs will become available. No longer will we have to scrape and scramble to feed our family. There are real jobs coming to our corner of the world.

As the factory is built, we join many of our neighbors for specialized training, getting prepared for a new career helping make a product we likely never saw or heard of. And pretty soon, we're part of a large operation to manufacture a modern product for sale in the global marketplace.

We may still be living in our hovel, but we can foresee the day when we will have saved enough money to move into the government housing complex now under construction near the factory, and we can hope for better lives for our children.

Along with the housing complex, new schools are being built – schools for our children – and we can envision brighter futures for our sons and daughters.

Back to America... We must help ourselves and our employees examine and understand this lifestyle of the people we are competing against, how it differs from our own, the lives of the people who work for our foreign competitors, the workers in foreign lands who do what we do.

Americans have a lifestyle that is the envy of the rest of the world. Is it in danger, threatened by people who today live in hovels, who aspire to government-built housing? Will these people, or their children and grandchildren be leading the lives of comfort and health comparable to that with which Americans have long been accustomed?

We need to better understand their lifestyle, and their aspirations, their history, culture, background, and what they bring with them to the twenty-first century. To what do they aspire? How much money do they make? What does that buy them? What are their benefits? Do they even get benefits?

We can educate ourselves by reading books about China and its recent history, by staying abreast of the news, and by viewing documentaries about modern China. Fact-based films, too, can enlighten us. I like the Chinese film, *"To Live."* The story follows the lives of a man and his wife through the turmoil of twentieth century

Chinese society: the Maoist revolution and the subsequent cultural revolutions and upheavals – from the 1940s through the 1970s to their old age, just prior to the nation's emergence into the modern world. They were survivors. These people, or rather their children and grandchildren, today, are our competitors.

In fact, their little granddaughter, who is born toward the end of the film, could well be a contemporary of Yu Shui, the central character in another excellent and relevant film, *"Up The Yangtze."* A fictional story of the impact of the Three Gorges Dam on the people of the Yangtze River valley, it shows how a young woman, Yu Shui, must take a job aboard a cruise ship to help her struggling family.

There, she enters into a dizzying microcosm of modern China. She's an unsophisticated country girl, swept up, confused, and overwhelmed by the sudden onslaught of modernity. Meanwhile, her parents face the rising waters of the Yangtze, dependent on the meager wages she sends home. The expanding lake behind the dam provides an apt metaphor for how modern China is overwhelming this modest peasant family (and many others).

Educating and exposing ourselves to this outside world by reading and staying abreast of cultural differences, watching such films and documentaries, is an important exercise. Yesterday, the Chinese were manufacturing cheap toys and trinkets. Today, they are making our smartphones, iPads, and computers – all of which were designed by Westerners. Tomorrow, no doubt, they will design, develop, and produce advanced jet aircraft and avionics, robotic medical devices, cutting-edge medicines, and numerous other innovative technologies – the very businesses that will have to drive America's future economy, too.

When we talk about change, it's not an abstract concept. Putting a human face on change helps people connect themselves to the change they must face. Stories like that of modern China and its impact on American business *are change*, the kind of change that is an unexpected slap in the face that says, "Wake up!"

But it need not be unexpected.

We all need better, more complete knowledge of what's driving China and its people as well as other developing nations like India, Brazil, the nations of Southeast Asia, and others in order to understand how best to prepare for and respond to this evolving and rapidly advancing competition. Only through those means will we be better prepared to share that understanding with our employees and, together, excel in our increasingly competitive world.

II. Organizations Are People

II. Organizations Are People

"Power consists in one's capacity to link his will with the purpose of others, to lead by reason and a gift of cooperation."

Woodrow Wilson

Maximize Your ROPI (Return on People Investment)

The core driver of any business lies in making investments with the expectation of positive (financial) returns. Companies build new factories and distribution centers, and buy machinery to establish the means to fabricate products and then get them to market. They spend a lot of money to extend product lines, expand into new markets, and create new products, all in the hope of realizing greater revenue and profits.

When customers in their target markets buy their products, the resulting revenue stream is what makes the up-front investments start paying off in the form of profit – also known as return on investment (ROI).

When business people talk about invested capital, this is what they generally mean: physical plants, equipment and transportation – the kinds of investments that are amortized and depreciated over time.

Building a new production plant may cost, say, $250 million (or far more) and the senior managers justify the expenditure to the board of directors on the basis of the projected ROI – how long it will take to "pay" for the investment before they can start realizing a profit on its output.

However, we rarely hear business people talk the same way about the investments they make in their people, and whether they are getting a good return on those investments. Employees can be an overlooked part of the big financial picture. That seems ironic, especially in light of the fact that the cost of personnel is often the biggest line item on most companies' balance sheets. In addition to salaries, health insurance premiums, and other benefits, investing in people includes many other things, such as:

- The time and money it takes to find the right person for a given position, including paying the recruiter and investing the dozens of hours that managers spend conducting interviews and winnowing down candidates to the final few.
- The initial and ongoing training necessary to assure that people acquire and sustain the skills needed to be the best they can in their jobs, and to excel and rise in the organization, further adding value.
- Various other costs incurred in retaining people, such as salary increases, incentives, bonuses, and other rewards.

This all may seem obvious. I only reiterate it here because of what we experienced starting in 2009. Millions of American jobs were lost – literally evaporated. Naturally, a good leader resorts to lay-offs only as a last option, doing so only after hiring and wage freezes, other expense cuts, and/or price increases have failed to stop the flow of red ink. They know that every single laid-off employee is a lost opportunity, a lost investment. Good leaders feel an ache in the pit of their stomach at the prospect of having to cut the work force.

While they are usually hyper-conscious of the personal side of each lay-off – the family that's impacted, and the blow to the employee's ego and sense of self-confidence – the business leader side of their personality also aches at the loss of investments of time and money. However, the bigger challenge and what keeps these leaders awake at night is what each lay-off does to the company and its future prospects. Yes, shedding jobs reduces expenses to better ensure the company's ability to persevere in the trying times – which is the point, after all.

But the care, feeding, and cultivation of effective employees are works in progress. When it all meshes and the company is thriving, there are few things that make a leader prouder than seeing the employees operating at their best, as a team, contributing collectively toward the company's mission – and, its profitability.

But when lay-offs are unavoidable, that finely tuned machine loses its edge. Remaining employees lose their focus on the mission. Instead, they become concerned for their own future with the company, wondering when the other shoe will drop.

That said, in the toughest times, businesses need to continue to cultivate their people to be sure they understand how much they mean to the future success of the business and how important it is for them to stay focused on the mission.

Of course, the key is communications – through both good times and bad. Keep employees well informed and actively engaged in the external challenges the company is facing: competitive threats, economic turmoil, government regulation and taxation, etc.

Share with them, too, the company's opportunities and always invite their perspective and ideas. Open and honest communications build trust and understanding, which will be what leadership needs most when the situation gets tough, when the best efforts of everyone and their full engagement to the company's mission becomes central to seeing it through hard times.

Reinforcing Values Drives the Right Behaviors

Most established companies are built on a set of values, underlining the business' core purpose and setting forth principles to guide their employees in the future to sustain the organization's health and success, regardless of who is in charge.

Values are not and never should be an after-thought. Rather, they should reinforce the vision and mission on which the company was created and built, as well as the attitudes and behaviors of its founders. If they are encouraged effectively, values can serve as fixed points of truth for succeeding generations of managers and employees to hold true to the founding principles of the business.

As a means of "living its core values" and reinforcing employee behavior that reflects those values, a former client company of mine conducted an annual contest among its employees. Each year, managers and supervisors would nominate individual employees or teams who they felt best exemplified in their work the meaning of the company's five core values: "customer focus," "honesty," "innovation," "respect for people," and "team spirit."

Each year, ahead of the year-end company holiday party where the awards were bestowed, the company president and the head of human resources would sit together, review the nominees, and select the most worthy teams and individuals in time to honor them at the annual party.

Winners would receive plaques and gift cards. It had become a well-established tradition of recognizing and rewarding the behavior that senior leadership sought. I remember thinking at the time that it was a grand idea because it put the spotlight on and rewarded the individuals and teams who were living, behaving, and acting the way the company had expected them to operate, in a manner that perpetuated the founding principles of the company.

I once got the opportunity to peruse the nomination papers and was impressed with the kinds of efforts people had made, and the wonderful ideas many had offered. Most of these people went beyond their nine-to-five routines and job responsibilities to extend themselves for the betterment of the company. There were instances of individual creativity that saved the company a lot of money and/or improved products and efficiencies, or customer services.

People do pay a lot of attention to how employees are rewarded and recognized. How else do you explain the plethora of entertainment and sports awards, as well as those in every other field? People like to acknowledge superior performance in any field. So these kinds of programs are a good idea.

It all seemed very inspiring and a good way to reinforce good work. But there was something about it that troubled me: the sense that it had become a predictable routine, and the realization that there would be winners every year.

It's a bit like the "Employee of the Month" plaques you see in the lobbies of many hotels and restaurants. With a finite number of employees, it's likely that everyone will eventually be honored. The first few times the award is given, everyone will generally agree that the selected winner is worthy of merit.

But by the time you're into the fourth or fifth year of the program, with 50 or 60 out of 75 or so employees having been honored, the award has lost much of its significance and meaning.

It becomes a case of diminishing returns.

Suppose the president of my client company had felt that none among the nominees were worthy of recognition? Would he decide not to give any awards that year? Would he be prepared to stand before the holiday gathering and say, "Sorry, nobody was worthy of the 'Core Values Honors' this year"? No. It's not going to happen – though it does happen in some realms. Occasionally, for instance, the Nobel Committee does not give a Nobel Prize for Literature or the Nobel Peace Prize – justifiably.

But skipping a year in what had become a company tradition like this "Core Values Honors" would have had a negative impact. So it continues year after year and inevitably begins to feel a bit tired and predictable. I don't mean to discourage this very appropriate recognition of outstanding service on the part of hard working employees, but organizations should be nimble and creative in how they do so. They should break out of the cookie-cutter expectations of an annual or monthly prize and be more spontaneous – and perhaps a bit unpredictable. Rewards and recognition are most meaningful when they occur randomly.

There's nothing wrong with flagging someone's outstanding work one day, and then highlighting someone else's three days later. Nor is there anything wrong with not recognizing anyone for a long stretch of several months, if no one merits the recognition. Taking that approach will have greater impact and meaning to people.

The important thing is to be paying attention to what the employees are doing, ready to provide constructive criticism, to help people be better at their jobs, at the same time, ready to say "thank you" or give a pat on the back when someone does a good job, or a significant reward and/or recognition when they do go above and beyond, especially when that effort embodies the values on which the organization was founded.

Perceptions and Perspectives

In both our personal and professional lives, we proceed through our days with perceptions of ourselves within the context of the larger world, and we act accordingly.

We have no other choice. Because we are only human, our unique point of view is necessarily limited by our perceptions: i.e., what our own five senses provide us in terms of information, input, and people's reactions to what we say and do.

On those occasions when we can expand our perspective by adding those of others, our point of view is broadened. And though we may not always be pleased or comfortable to learn these kinds of truths, our ability to live in the world and work with other people has nevertheless been significantly expanded and improved.

The same holds true in corporate communications. At the start of a new assignment, our client liaison provides us an overview of the company and the challenges and opportunities her/his company faces – in particular, the challenges and opportunities for which we have been retained to help address.

Yet, as well informed as she/he may be, the liaison can give us but one perspective. It's not surprising, then, that our best work happens when we are able to launch new assignments with the benefit of additional perspectives and insights, which we do through a number of means, not the least of which is talking to as many people as possible, both inside and outside the organization. This is not to say that the liaison is wrong or ill informed. In fact, our client contacts are usually among the best informed in the companies we work with, because they're usually in a senior communications role, which demands that they stay well connected and current across all functions and departments.

Even so, the perspective of one person who resides in one part of any organization is necessarily limited and influenced by where that person sits and whom she/he listens to and respects.

Even the CEO is not immune to this shortcoming. In my years of working with a range of corporate leaders, some have been very conscious of this challenge of perceptions and perspectives, and effective at dealing with it directly. Others have not, carrying an arrogant attitude that says, "I know what the truth is."

The CEO of a former client, a global airline, made it a central part of his job to reach out regularly to the company's many stakeholders: employees, paying customers, FAA regulators, stockholders, industry analysts, etc.

Once, we were visiting their headquarters building and, when we went to lunch in the company cafeteria, I spotted the CEO sitting at a table with a half-dozen employees. When I remarked on it, my host said that that was the CEO's habit when he was in the headquarters office. He would simply pull up a chair at a table and dine with employees. He would talk to them, listen a lot, answer their questions, and test ideas with them.

We were told that he did the same when he traveled, always building into his schedule sufficient time at the airports around the world to talk to ground crews, customer service reps, and aircraft crewmembers.

He flew both coach and first class, and quizzed adjacent passengers about their experiences with the airline, while striving to remain incognito to elicit honest customer insights.

As it is with us when we start an assignment by immersing ourselves in multiple perspectives, a CEO like this one is going to be smarter and better connected to the core truths of his organization, as well as the ways in which it evolves.

He will often sense impending challenges or changes before anyone else does. He has no illusions about the forces that impact the health of his company, and doesn't have to be dependent on a buffer zone of advisors, assistants and yes-men. Consequently, he can operate more effectively, and make better-informed and timelier decisions based on reality.

There's an additional advantage of his reaching out. Because he makes the ongoing effort to extend himself and listen to his company's key stakeholders, he operates with their support and trust – which is perhaps his greatest asset in doing his job and seeing the company through rough patches.

This holds true whenever we seek to broaden our own self-perception by folding in additional perspectives. When we do so, we envelope greater truths beyond our own world view and bring ourselves closer to the ultimate reality, building greater trust among our peers along the way.

Does a Collaborative Culture Require Proximity?

At the start of her tenure in early 2013, Yahoo's then-new CEO Marissa Mayer made headlines and stirred controversy and discussion, both inside the company and out, when she issued her edict that effectively ended all employees' work-from-home. At the time, a stumbling Yahoo needed to rebuild the culture it had lost over the years. Mayer's prescription was to create a more collaborative environment, which could only happen, she insisted, if everyone is in the office every day.

Her industry peers at companies like Google and Apple at the time appeared to agree. Nearly the same time as Mayer's edict, Google introduced its Frank Gehry-designed "Bayview" expansion of its Googleplex headquarters in Mountain View, a key feature of which was that no individual employee would be more than a two-and-a-half-minute walk from any other staffer.

The idea, according to a spokesman at the time, was that such proximity encourages and builds collaborative behaviors and spontaneity that, in turn, lead to greater innovation and creativity.

Before his death, Steve Jobs similarly talked about the importance and value of collaboration and chance encounters between employees.

In the context of introducing the design for Apple's new (yet to be built) headquarters to the Cupertino city council for their zoning approval, he said that some of the best ideas to come out of Apple were the result of spontaneous encounters and conversations in the hallways and break rooms. A similar compulsion drove his design of Pixar's offices across the bay in Emeryville. The huge circular, spaceship-like design of the proposed Apple's new headquarters would accomplish the same thing, he insisted.

A collaborative culture is one where engaged employees work as one toward a common purpose. People bring their unique skills and backgrounds together as a team or unit and contribute collectively toward a greater outcome, to fulfill the organization's vision.

Conversely, where the notion of collaboration is foreign, employees compete with one another, resulting in dysfunction and redundancies. In a collaborative culture, the organization realizes multiple benefits, including:

- Greater clarity about what is needed for success
- Inclusive decision-making
- Fresh thinking and innovative solutions
- Efficient, concerted actions in the service of shared, measurable goals
- Effective time management
- Greater trust, and broader engagement

So, is physical proximity a requirement of effective collaboration? Ironically, the same day as Mayer's announcement, the Census Bureau released a study that showed a steady rise in the number of people engaged in at-home work today in America. Some 13.4 million people – about 9.4% of the workforce – worked at least one day per week at home in 2010, an increase over 1997 data that showed seven percent of the workforce did.

Case in point, employees at a client company of ours, in 2013, moved into a gleaming new, glass-encased headquarters building. Subsequently, they had to adapt to their company's new concept of the "workplace." The building was designed for 110% occupancy. So no one has a permanently assigned desk, office or landline phone number.

Rather, people – including the CEO and his senior management team – work in large, open areas at long tables among their function or department peers, using laptops and mobile phones wherever they may sit on a given day. Adjacent glass-enclosed rooms of varying sizes are available for private meetings or conference calls. There are also smaller one-person rooms for private phone calls.

The design is a physical manifestation of the evolution of the modern workplace, acknowledging that people do work from home on occasion. Others travel. The building design team's analysis said it could safely anticipate that all employees would never show up on any given day. Why accommodate them all every day?

But in such cases – which we know have become the norm – is collaboration possible without every employee being walking distance from one another, as some insist? Enter modern technology, which is largely responsible for allowing people such freedom in choosing where they work.

Achieving a collaborative way of life within an organization where everyone is under the same roof is one thing. It's an altogether different matter when people are scattered around the globe or across the country in multiple locations – even without any work-from-home employees.

Web and video conferencing enables real-time virtual face-to-face conferences, bringing the additional advantage of seeing people's faces while we talk with them, enabling everyone to catch the subtleties of facial inflections, like smiles and frowns, that add meaning to one's words. It also enables the group simultaneously to examine documents under discussion.

Similarly, webinars facilitate online collaboration for larger groups and company-wide meetings such as leadership town halls and "All Hands" meetings. Webinar leaders – be it the CEO, a division head or an internal expert or external consultant – can present research findings, new initiatives, new products, new ideas, or new approaches. Some webinar solutions offer recording and archiving functions that enable employees who want a second viewing or who may have missed the initial meeting the opportunity to view the recording at their leisure.

If used regularly by all team members, internal social media like Yammer or Jive can also stimulate and sustain collaboration, regardless of employees' proximity to one another.

So while we understand Marissa Mayer's desire to bring all Yahoo employees back to headquarters, improved collaboration can't be seen as the real reason. Rather, the real motive is more likely her need to bring some order to a chaotic situation.

Collaboration happens not because people have been forced into a single common location, but rather because a conscious decision was made to make it happen, and then the right things were done to help sustain it.

As a concurrent *New York Times* article noted several paragraphs deep, Yahoo had become a company "where employees were aimless and morale was low." Mayer's immediate fix was physical proximity. Time will tell whether it was the right approach. Any improvement in collaboration would be a bonus of, but not a rationale for her action.

The Internal Value of Corporate Philanthropy

Perhaps out of a sense of obligation (i.e., "everyone else does it and so should we"), major public corporations are usually generous with their philanthropy, funding everything from local and national arts and cultural institutions, to pure science and medical research, and education, as well as established charitable organizations.

Often this kind of corporate giving reflects the organization's business, such as a medical device manufacturer or pharmaceutical company giving money to medical research and teaching hospitals. No one questions the legitimacy or value of such munificence. But what many businesspeople fail to ask is whether their company's philanthropic gifts bring a good return on investment for the company and its stakeholders.

In other words, are businesses realizing full value for their philanthropy? I would bet that a survey of businesses would discover that the answer is most often "I don't know," or "What do you mean by that?"

When asked why their organizations engage in their chosen philanthropies, many company spokespeople fumble for an answer – as though they had never contemplated the question – and offer only vague responses along the lines of "to be a responsible member of the community," or "to give something back."

That's all well and good, and I would never criticize or question that as the motive for giving. But I dare say they aren't communicating anything like that internally, and I doubt that many of their employees could verbalize the rationale for their company's corporate giving.

Certainly philanthropy – "giving something back" – is admirable, but stockholders and directors expect to see returns on the investments their companies make. Beyond the mere tax break it may give them, charitable giving is no exception. As cynical as that may sound, I suggest that there are valuable returns to the donors, but that many companies either are not strategic about their giving, not cognizant of the returns, not fully exploiting their philanthropy, or not measuring its impact.

In some instances, customers implicitly or explicitly demand charitable giving as a precondition to doing business with individual companies. So philanthropy in such cases may be seen as the price of admission to certain markets. Those types of returns are numerous, but the ones I concern myself with here center on the most important stakeholder audience: employees. How are companies leveraging their philanthropic efforts to better engage their employees in the business? What are the near- and long-term internal benefits to be realized through corporate philanthropy?

One Midwestern manufacturer (a former client) provides an excellent case study. The company makes it a policy to take an active role in the many cities and towns in which it has plants. One city (where its local facility employs some six-thousand locals) once had a reputation for crime and poverty – before the company got involved.

Over the course of several years of determined involvement and significant monetary grants, the company played an integral role in turning the city around. Year-over-year declining crime statistics proved its impact. The company's manager in charge of community involvement told me that all employees were encouraged to choose community efforts and activities in which to be involved – sometimes on company time. In some instances, the employees themselves identified those projects and, in turn, solicited the company for necessary funding.

Employees were recognized and often rewarded by the company for their community involvement and what they were able to achieve as individual contributors or members of teams helping out in community efforts.

Examples of these activities included the renovation of city parks and recreation facilities, hands-on involvement in the local Head Start program, anti-crime work in cooperation with the local police department, and the creation and maintenance of an educational nature center and preserve. Though the manager didn't say so, I think that the company has realized some important long-term benefits among its employees. Knowing that their employer was investing in, supporting and encouraging community involvement and out-reach no doubt increased their pride in, and loyalty and commitment to the company.

By extension, we can assume that an employee working on the production line, for instance, came to understand that the quality of his/her effort would have a direct and positive impact on the company's bottom line and, therefore, its ability to continue being a contributing member of the very community in which the employee and her/his family live.

In other words, if employees can see the direct link between their contributions to the success of the company and its ability to give back to the community, they win and their community wins. Not only are employees sustaining their families with a steady paycheck from this company; this company is helping to improve the lives of the employee, his/her family, and neighbors. And that's quite a return on an investment, no matter how you measure it.

Uncertainty Dims Company Morale

Caught up in the sub-prime mortgage fiasco, followed by the worst economy of modern times, commercial banks were particularly hard-hit in 2008 and 2009. Then, the new "Dodd–Frank Wall Street Reform and Consumer Protection Act" squeezed them further. Subsequently, it seemed that their every attempt to add or increase a fee on its services induced howls of indignation from customers and industry watchdogs.

With little near-term hope of improving their bottom line, the big players like Citigroup, Wells Fargo and Bank of America began looking under every figurative and literal rock to find savings, as well as ways to improve revenues and profits. Apparently finding insufficient new revenue and savings, Bank of America CEO Brian Moynihan announced one day in the summer of 2011 that overall employment levels at the bank "would be reduced by thirty-thousand over the next few years."

If you had been an employee of Bank of America at that time and read that, which part of that statement would bother you most? Would it have been the fact that thirty-thousand people at your company are likely going to lose their jobs, including maybe you? Or is it the implicit uncertainty as to when the axe might fall? For me, it would be the latter.

I think sure knowledge of impending doom is preferable to uncertainty that something bad will occur at some undetermined point in the future. It's akin to being a pre-adolescent, in trouble with

Mom one afternoon for breaking a window, and then hearing her ominous threat, "Just you wait until your father gets home!" It's a postponement of the Judgment Day. Anticipating the paddling you'd get a few hours hence was pretty scary. I remember hoping that my dad would come home in a forgiving mood and just give me a "good talking-to."

The lead sentence in the *Wall Street Journal* article that reported the impending cuts got my award for understatement of the year: "Morale quickly turns ugly after a company warns about layoffs – even if the job cuts won't happen for a while." I would change that to read: "...*especially* if the job cuts won't happen for a while." One analyst quoted in the article said that he didn't know "anybody who's not looking for another job" there. No surprise. That would be a natural reaction to such gross uncertainty.

The trouble is, in a lousy economy, there are not thirty-thousand open jobs out there to which those people could jump just for the asking. So they likely sat at their Bank of America jobs, and they were not very happy. And they were not likely feeling too loyal toward Bank of America. Even if the axe didn't ultimately fall on them, the weeks and months of anticipation made them less productive and less engaged employees.

From the *Journal* article, we also learned that managers had "tried to send short notes to reassure employees, but it seems they are nervous about their own positions." No kidding. How can you, as a manager, encourage your employees to have confidence in and trust the institution when you don't yourself, when you are suffering the same anxieties and uncertainty as they are?

Look, I understand that Moynihan was as much in the dark as anyone else about the state of the economy going forward and whether the fortunes of his bank would improve over the next quarter or even the next year. He couldn't very well enact immediate job cuts, lest it make the organization non-functional and further worsen its business case. But at the same time, he created a self-fulfilling prophecy of doom.

In such circumstances, even his most talented people were not going to be at their best, focused less on the job at hand than on whether and when the HR manager would come knocking on their door, accompanied by the security officer come to walk them out the door.

He didn't ask me, but if Moynihan had wanted my advice, I'd have told him to hold this one closer to the vest. The *Journal* article quotes an analyst speculating that he made the announcement to mollify Wall Street. I sure hope not. It wouldn't have made much sense if that had been his purpose. In that climate, BAC stock was already getting hammered, hitting historic lows. And the announcement didn't cause so much as an upward blip in the price.

It would have been far better had he worked through the implications of near- and long-term strategies regarding job cuts – if, in fact, he and his executive team determined that to be the wisest path. Clearly, a cut of such magnitude (representing more than 10 percent of the total workforce) implies some drastic changes in the way the bank will conduct business going forward.

Perhaps they were planning to get out of some businesses, or maybe some geographic areas. Likely they anticipated closing branches and some back-office operations. That's where his public statements ought to have been focused: on the business changes he was considering.

It is near impossible for a company the size of Bank of America to inform the internal audience before going public. So there should have been a concerted effort to inform the affected employees concurrent with the public announcement, providing them with as much information as possible while answering as many questions as they could. A dismal internal morale had already permeated Bank of America. There wasn't much he could have said that would have changed that.

But having the CEO operate with greater certainty and sense of urgency is far more effective in retaining employee focus and commitment than the aura of uncertainty that Moynihan cast with his broadcast announcement. The company was going to need as much employee focus and commitment as it could get if it was ever going to be successful again.

The Futile Pursuit of "Perfect" in Job Postings

When unemployment rates are persistently high, the job market is a buyer's market. Because of that, people who may be unhappy or feel frustrated with their current situations are stuck, reluctant to leave for fear that they won't find another position elsewhere.

This double-edged sword changes the nature of many workplaces and the inter-relations there, while stifling the vital organizational renewal that the ebb and flow of natural attrition in normal times brings organizations, with new employees coming in and established (sometimes stale) employees leaving.

With little movement of people out of organizations (except in cases of lay-offs or retirements), postings for the rare openings in such periods become pursuits of perfection. Requirements can often be absurdly detailed and lengthy, virtual shopping lists of specific ideal talents, skills and experience.

That's fine for highly technical jobs where familiarity and facility with various technologies, equipment and/or computer software is necessary. But for those positions that require intellectual curiosity, agility, and creativity, as well as an ability to work well with a variety of people, there is no ideal job description.

Still, the employers advertising for many such positions apparently operate under the delusion that "perfect" is attainable. An article in *The Wall Street Journal* in mid-2012 reported on a study that found that thirty-one percent of the 811 small businesses surveyed had unfilled job openings in the previous month because they couldn't identify applicants "with the right skills or experience." In an opinion piece, "Mind The Gap," in *The New Yorker* that ran at about the same time, author James Surowiecki cited the "dearth of qualified workers... and the gap between the skills that American workers have and the ones that businesses need."

That's recruiter talk. I contend that, in the pursuit of the perfect, employers may overlook the *right* candidate. Working from the notion that there is the perfect candidate out there creates an insurmountable barrier to the applicant who, in the light of day, could be the best fit for the team and contribute the most to the greater good of the organization.

Unfortunately, the resume screening software in wide use today seeks the perfect candidate, but makes no accommodation for anything except the candidates that match nearly the entire shopping list. So, as the *Journal* article notes, positions go unfilled.

On the other hand, the right candidate is going to be the one that comes with her/his own unique skills, talents, abilities and intelligence that may or may not fulfill all the specificity outlined in the job posting.

While the job certainly has its roles and responsibilities, in addition to fulfilling those, the right candidate will also ultimately make the position distinctively his/her own, reflecting his/her unique personality, approach, and talent mix. In the long term, the team and the organization will be stronger for it.

But, in actual practice, the job description is treated like a monolithic beast, falsely assuming that the job is like the glass slipper in the fairy tale "Cinderella." Only the single perfect foot will fit. Rather, the job description should be a broad outline of desirable skills and background, leaving the ultimate selection to the discerning eye of the hiring manager.

This paradox is compounded by businesses' own reluctance to prepare new people fully and properly for the job. Both the *Journal* and *New Yorker* articles note that, to an increasing degree, businesses are loath to invest in training, on the (*very false*) assumption that the perfect candidate is ready to go full speed on Day 1.

As Surowiecki noted, the ultimate irony of a weak economy is that "most companies worry less about getting every possible dollar of new business than they do about keeping costs down. That makes them slow to hire, which keeps unemployment high, which keeps the economy weak, which in turn makes employers more reluctant to hire," adding that they are similarly disinclined to hire anyone who needs the least bit of training because of the attendant time and money investments.

When unemployment rates are persistently stuck at high levels, employers can afford to be choosey, willing to wait to find that one unique needle in the haystack of resumes.

While they make little accommodation for training, they also likely don't provide chances for the new hire to gain an understanding of and appreciation for the company's culture, how things work, or anything much more than learning where the washrooms, lunch room, and parking lot are.

Onboarding becomes a cursory affair of filling out forms and handing out policy manuals. "Just do your job. Oh, and by the way, do it at a salary less than your last job."

And yet, they still get thousands upon thousands of applications. What does this do to the workplace? What kinds of employees begin to populate an organization like this? How do the older, more established employees – those who may consider themselves "stuck" – feel toward and about the newbies who are working for less money? Are there still time and opportunities for camaraderie, for personal moments and friendliness any more? What's increasingly missing today is the notion that new people come into a company, feel their way around a bit, find their niche, and establish their own style and unique contribution to the larger whole in their own distinctive way.

People should be allowed to grow into a job. They should be able to learn and understand what their role entails, the nature and heritage of the company and its values, how the business works, its customers, and the idiosyncrasies of their new boss. Given that opportunity, they feel encouraged to bring fresh insights to old challenges – all for the betterment of the company.

Instead, we have an expectation that new hires will attain the necessary insights and understanding to do the job – through osmosis or ESP, I suppose – and do so quickly because there's no time to waste. Everybody is "slammed," running between back-to-back meetings, with no time to help teach the new guy the ropes.

I've seen it first-hand, where newcomers show up for work and their new boss is on the road for two weeks, leaving no one responsible for a little friendliness and onboarding into the new job and department.

I hope that it is not an anachronism to believe that people can grow into the job. I also hope that it's not wrong to support the notion that every job is unique to the person who holds it, that people can mold the job to their special skills, insights, and style and thus contribute far more to the greater strength of the team and the advancement of the organization and its mission.

Life Lessons Learned on Playing Fields

As a schoolboy, like many other kids, I played Little League baseball. In high school, I ran cross-country and track. Mind you, I was never a star athlete. My baseball career ended when I was too old for Little League. And my long distance running times were mediocre, at best. That's not to say I didn't enjoy myself or get a lot out of the experiences. I'm still a rabid baseball fan, and I continued running recreationally into my adult years, including training for and competing in a half-dozen marathons.

Aside from the fun of competition, the three key lessons I learned from participating in sports were deep and have stayed with me to this day. It's why I feel strongly that children should be encouraged to compete in sports – aside from the obvious health benefits.

Lesson number one is the importance of preparation. Second is tenacity. Lastly is what we learn by being a member of a team.

The best ballplayers in the Major Leagues are the ones you see on the field before every game taking batting practice. Even the veterans. Especially the veterans. They take multiple swings. Meanwhile, the best infielders will field countless grounders in practice.

In my brief high school career in cross-country and track, our best runner always ran both before and after school – even in the off-season. When we finished our after-school practice, he'd keep running. The rest of us were too exhausted from our workouts and never felt the urge to join him in his extended runs. He was singularly dedicated. As a senior, he won the California state cross-country championship in the fall and went on to win the mile in the state track and field championship. I wasn't surprised, though I was certainly impressed.

The same holds true in business. We do our best work and feel most confident when we know what we're talking about – and I mean *really know* it. Conversely, when we come into a meeting without previewing materials, without preparing, without thinking through the purpose of the meeting and our role, we often make fools of ourselves. Worse, we waste other people's time.

It's a lesson we learn in Little League, and other youth sports. If you showed up for a game having missed practice, chances are the coach was not going to let you play – not as punishment, but because he was pretty sure that you weren't ready.

Being involved in sports also teaches you to be persistent. Clearing a given height in high jump or pole vault is an immediate goal. After failing on the initial try, true competitors don't stop. They give it another go. Same with the miler, the shortstop, or the running back when their efforts fall short.

I would take third place (or worse) in the mile at a track meet, running slower than I knew I was capable of. My coach always spoke encouraging words after such performances and helped me appreciate my true abilities.

I came away with a desire to go back the next time with renewed determination, a resolve to practice harder, and a yearning to push myself harder during the next race through the pain that had held me back.

Again, it's an important lesson for business, where we may fail to win an account, or fall short of performance metrics. But we don't quit. Instead, we carefully examine what we did that led to the less-than-satisfactory outcome and make appropriate adjustments for future such endeavors. And that generally means putting in a more strenuous effort and, likely, more time.

While the foregoing lessons are valuable, perhaps the most important one learned as an adolescent team member is one's role as a contributor to a larger entity. Though every team has its standout members, the collective unit, as a whole, succeeds on the sum total contribution of all its members. Superstars in team sports cannot beat the other teams alone without her/his teammates and their varied contributions.

Similarly, no business succeeds on the genius and drive of its founder and/or leadership team, or an individual contributor. Instead, it depends on the collective genius and efforts of many people at all levels of the organization, each doing her/his job well, each consistently striving for excellence in their own area of responsibility, each focused on business goals.

Our individual knowledge and awareness of our unique role and responsibilities as part of the larger operation is critical to the organization's succeeding or failing. The best leaders are those that not only communicate the importance of the individuals' contributions and the significance of their excellence, but also really comprehend and appreciate its value, and lead the team accordingly, identifying and addressing overall weaknesses.

In the end, aren't we all striving for the level of performance we sought in our youth sports? Isn't our role as members of a business team ultimately an extension of the roles when we played on our Little League team? Those were valuable lessons we learned as kids, and we'd be wise to think of them not only as nostalgic memories but also as life lessons to hold dearly.

Walking the Management Tightrope

Being a manager is to walk a tightrope. It's about finding and maintaining the right balance consistently, lest you fall and fail. By balance, I mean walking that fine line between over-managing people and giving them too much leeway in their jobs. I couldn't illustrate this truth better than did Danish novelist Carsten Jensen in a passage in his well-crafted 2011 novel, "We, The Drowned," a multi-layered story of generations of seamen from the small Danish port of Marstal:

> *"Every sailing ship has miles of ropes, scores of blocks, hundreds of square yards of canvas. Unless the ropes are constantly pulled and the sails endlessly adjusted, the ship becomes a helpless victim of the wind. Managing a crew is the same thing.*

> *"The captain holds hundreds of invisible ropes in his hands. Allowing the crew to take charge is letting the wind take the helm: the ship will be wrecked. But if the captain takes complete control, the ship will be becalmed and go nowhere: he strips his men of all initiative; they'll no longer do their best and go about their work with reluctance. It's all a question of experience and knowledge. But first and foremost, it's about authority."*

Of course, modern organizations are not nineteenth century sailing vessels. Plying the vast open waters of the world's great oceans at the mercy of fickle winds, currents and weather, there was an ever-

present danger of rogue waves, sudden storms and typhoons, and lapses in judgment that could and often did result in disaster: lost ships, drowned crew, and lost cargo.

While there may be no such life-and-death dangers in today's modern office buildings and factory floors, the metaphor works. Managers who keep a tight rein on their teams, who micro-manage and second-guess their employees' every move, soon create a disheartened workforce. I've seen these situations first-hand. Employees "check out." They go through the motions of doing their jobs, waiting for their manager to correct them, rebuke them, or figuratively reach over their shoulders and do their jobs for them.

This approach begs the question of such managers: why do you hire people? And exactly what skills were you looking for when you hired them? Are your people interchangeable? Clearly, by their actions, this sort of manager telegraphs gross insecurity that often betrays a personal lack of confidence, an innate craving to be superior when, in fact, that is in doubt.

Conversely, the other extreme can be just as bad. When the manager is hands-off, offering little or no feedback or coaching, employees are cut adrift. They are left to guess what is expected of them, what determines excellence. In their minds, what they do has little meaning. Their errors and mistakes may or may not bring harm to the company, but it's unlikely they'll realize it until it's too late.

The happy middle ground is a bit of both: mentoring and coaching, nurturing and building the self-assurance of one's employees until they feel secure and confident in their own abilities.

They eventually gain a larger understanding of the team's challenges, better able to make independent judgments, acquiring the wisdom that comes with experience. As Jensen notes, a manager's role is to exert authority – not by doing your team members' jobs for them or second-guessing every decision they make, but rather by driving them to improve their own individual performances constantly for the betterment of the larger effort. It is coaching them to ask the right questions and to strive for personal improvement in their individual quests for excellence.

As a manager, it's your responsibility to leverage your own knowledge and experiences to guide and coach your employees toward the acquisition of the same in application to the unit's and the business' challenges. It is helping them make the connections between what they do every day and the organization's larger purpose and goals.

To resume the metaphor, it is teaching, coaching and encouraging them, and then overseeing their correct deployment of sails, lines and rudder, rather than doing it for them.

Peering Behind the Ad Agency Curtain

The daily interactions between people that occur in any workplace shape that organization's culture, and make it a desirable place to work – or not. The daily struggle to create and maintain quality products and/or services is always a push-pull between people with different viewpoints, and sometimes opposing senses of what will work and what won't.

This is especially true in an advertising agency, where the sum total of the firm's worth lies in its ability to operate as a team to deliver strategically targeted, consistently high quality creative work, which in turn must effectively sell its clients' goods and services.

"The Pitch," a weekly TV series that ran for a couple of seasons a few years ago on AMC, attempted to give us a peek behind the curtain inside the world of advertising agencies. Based on my own career in the business, my impression was that it did an okay job of it within the confines of a one-hour time slot interspersed with commercials.

Filmed like most other reality TV shows with ever-present cameras in participants' faces, the premise of the show pitted two ad agencies against one another in pursuit of a new, very real piece of business.

There was much truth in the broadcast: the tension, the petty jealousies, the short fuses, the preening egos, the long hours of work, the frustrations of false starts, and the prickliness. But there was also the whirlwind excitement of throwing crazy ideas against the wall in the hope that one would stick and ultimately become the killer idea that won the account. And then there was the jubilation and profound sense of relief that comes with winning the account, versus the crestfallen losers licking their wounds.

Like most reality TV shows, the primary focus was on the interactions between people, the quest for the right chemistry, both between the agency and its prospective client, as well as internally within the agency among the people who work long hours under a tight deadline to deliver winning work.

"The Pitch" does a great job of capturing that tension, the sleepless nights and long days, and the death spiral feeling during the final days and hours leading up to "the pitch." We're reminded with on-screen captions how many days or hours are left as the creative teams scramble in the wee hours of the morning to put the finishing touches on the idea they hope will win.

The show's first episode pitted WDCW of Los Angeles against McKinney of Durham, NC, for the Subway breakfast account. The prospective client, headquartered in Milford, CT, meant that both agencies had to fly considerable distances to meet (jointly, simultaneously and awkwardly) their prospective client who outlined the assignment. They each returned a week later with hoped-for knock-their-socks-off ideas to close the deal. (By the way, that's an unrealistically tight deadline. But this is television.)

As the story unfolded, Subway had already expanded the hours its outlets were open in order to serve breakfast. But executives were unsatisfied with sales results. So this assignment would target a younger demographic – eighteen- to twenty-four-year-olds – which they believed held the most promise for growth.

The Chief Marketing Officer at Subway was the guy who would ultimately judge the winner. I didn't envy the competitors because he seemed like a tough customer able to maintain a good poker face. The sense of panic set in immediately back in their home shops. McKinney roped in its younger staff because they were members of the target demographic. These kids looked like they'd been out of college for a couple of minutes. Their ideas were rough, but intriguing. A key element of the process that was missing from the broadcast – probably because it's not as sexy as the creative process – was the strategizing that always occurs before any creative work can begin. Let's assume it happened off-camera. That component would have included the following questions:

- Who's the target audience – specifically and generally?
- What do we know about them and their breakfast preferences?
- What are their media preferences?
- There's an implicit assumption from the get-go that the creative product will be TV advertising, which assumes the target audience watches TV. If so, how do they watch: with finger poised over mute buttons at commercial breaks? At what time of day do they watch? What shows or types of shows do they watch?
- What kinds of peer pressures determine their buying habits and dining preferences?
- What excites them, and what turns them off?

Answering these and related questions guide the media planning and strategy that help center the creative effort and avoid the problem of ineffective advertising down the road. But we were left assuming that these agencies apparently just skipped ahead, riding forward confidently on their assumptions. McKinney's chief creative officer was an unsmiling killjoy who seemed to like none of his team's ideas. While bullying them, he delighted in knocking down a lot of plausible approaches while offering no guidance or suggestions. Perhaps that was his style, but for a business that thrives on good relationships among team members, his methods struck me as cold and counter-productive.

"The Pitch" spent more time on McKinney – probably because they were the ultimate winners. We got a good flavor of the creative back-and-forth that lies at the heart of the ad business: the kicking around of crazy ideas in a conference room and the excitement when something feels *just right*.

The winning idea involved a rapper, Mac Lethal, who wrote a clever rap lyric that the McKinney team videotaped in a local Subway shop. McKinney went one step further, bringing the rapper to the pitch. As they closed their presentation, he entered the room, surprising the client, and rapped his praises for Subway. The client grinned for the first time.

The closing scenes accurately portrayed the results back at their home offices – the McKinney offices exploding into cheers at the news, while the WDCW team played basketball and talked philosophically, though not credibly, about not having "played to win."

It's an entertaining reality TV show, but not the full story. It glamorized the business, as seemed to be its intent, with none of the downside of working in an ad agency: the slow-paying clients and subsequent cash flow problems, the lost accounts, and the impossible-to-please clients. Take shows like "The Pitch" with a big grain of salt and enjoy them as typical reality TV shows.

But also appreciate shows like "The Pitch" for showing how people in difficult business situations can work together to win.

III. Employee Engagement

III. Employee Engagement

"It's not just recruiting. After recruiting, it's then building an
environment that makes people feel
they are surrounded by equally talented people
and their work is bigger than they are."

Steve Jobs

Employee Engagement is a Two-Way Street

The responsibility of keeping employees well informed about and engaged in the business is a mutual one.

Yes, it is critical that company leadership and managers communicate regularly and maintain an ongoing dialogue with employees to ensure that they understand, comprehend and act on the challenges and opportunities that confront the business.

But, at the same time, it is just as important for the individual employee to take the initiative to stay engaged in, be curious about, and stay informed about the business: what makes it tick, its history and heritage, its internal and external challenges and opportunities, and its paths to success.

That said, I surprised myself a couple years ago when I momentarily forgot this little truth. I had the honor of delivering a webinar on behalf of Citrix Online and Ziff-Davis on the subject of keeping a distributed workforce engaged and connected to the business. It was done as a companion piece to a white paper I'd prepared for them on the same subject.

As the date of the webinar approached, I was polishing my presentation, which focused mostly on what I was told the audience would be most interested in: techniques and new technologies for communicating with remote employees and keeping them informed and engaged, topics that I did indeed cover. Belatedly, I realized I was forgetting one important element – which I added almost as an after-thought to my presentation. In talking about the attitudes and behaviors that leaders and managers must exhibit toward a distributed workforce, as well as the communications techniques, messages and tools that organizations must use to reach them, it occurred to me that there are two sides to that coin.

Yes, it is incumbent upon communicators, managers and leaders to make every possible effort to keep employees in the loop and engaged in the business, no matter where they are. It is one of their most important roles. And doing so with employees who are not, as a rule, in the main office but rather working from afar in a remote office, or working from home, presents additional communications challenges. Yet it is even more critical because distributed employees can become easily disengaged.

But this is a two-way street, as I told my audience. The burden of staying connected and engaged in the business is just as much a responsibility of the individual employee as it is her/his employer. So the natural question arises: how do you instill in employees the urge to stay engaged and informed? And is that the responsibility of managers and leaders? Frankly, it should be self-motivated, something employees desire, a part of their natural urge to succeed, and to grow and progress in the organization.

If I were to give a speech to a college graduating class, I would tell them that if they're going into business and want to get ahead, they must stay engaged in the enterprise itself at least as much as their own role. While they learn their job, master its intricacies, and do the job well, they must, at the same time, strive to understand the details of what drives the business. In fact, they must make a concerted effort always to connect their role to the larger mission of the organization.

Managers, whether consciously or not, gravitate toward those employees who are fully engaged in the business over and above their own narrow role and responsibilities. These are the employees that managers are eager to hire and promote – as opposed to the clock-punchers, the folks who are out the door at five o'clock, regardless of what's still on their desks.

Comparing the two types of employees, it becomes obvious which is going to contribute more to the company's strategies and ultimate successes: the one that connects consistently what she/he does every day with where the company is going, the one whose individual efforts always support the organization's larger purpose.

Nurture Your Internal Champions

Over the years, through numerous client assignments involving a range of industries, company size and business focus, I've seen a pattern repeated in virtually every sizable organization for which I've done work. In the course of trying to get employees engaged in the organization's mission, vision and values, or to get them on board for a new initiative, employees can be roughly categorized into one of three types. These types may be familiar to you. You may use different terms to describe them and feel that my percentage break-down is a bit off, but I trust our views closely parallel one another.

At the top of the hierarchy are those I call the "Eager Beavers." These are the ones who "get it." You don't need to convince them when it comes to enacting the necessary changes to make an initiative succeed. They readily understand the rationale and its links to the corporate mission and the business' success.

They know what underpins the organization, the imperatives that are driving it, and how they personally fit into the larger whole. They can readily draw the connection between what they do every day and where the company needs to go. Eager Beavers want to do well, and they want to progress up the corporate ladder because they believe in the company and its mission. Generally speaking, because of their positive attitude, these people do, in fact, get promoted.

Whether you realize it or not, these are the ones for whom you provide the bulk of the information you generate. When their manager explains a new initiative in a group meeting, she/he might refer their team to the company's intranet website where additional background information is provided. The Eager Beavers are the ones who invariably go to that web page to learn more. And they may well read everything that's posted there.

Conversely, at the bottom of the hierarchy is what I call the "Disconnecteds." These are the employees you'll likely not reach – no matter what you do. They rarely pay attention to corporate messages unless they're affected directly, such as layoff notices or benefit changes. They don't bother to stay abreast of the outside competitive environment and what's impacting the company. They're likely just showing up every day for the paycheck. You know the type.

In most organizations, each of these two segments is roughly the same size, each of them anywhere from 10 to 20 percent of the total employee population. If your company is lucky, the percent of Eager Beavers exceeds that of the Disconnecteds.

I contend that strategic communications programs will have little or no impact on the Eager Beavers or the Disconnecteds, either in making the Eager Beavers more engaged – who, frankly, couldn't be more engaged – or in finally engaging the Disconnecteds.

Sure, our messages reach the Eager Beavers, and they likely gobble up every word, while the Disconnecteds ignore most of it or, at best, give it a cursory perusal. But even if our communications are lacking, count on the Eager Beavers to find out on their own, while, conversely, your best communications efforts will not reach the Disconnecteds in a way that will change their behaviors.

So our communications efforts should target the "Big Middle," the 50 to 70 percent of the people who might be convinced of the value of buying into the new change initiative, the corporate mission, or a new strategy. Our challenge as communicators is finding the right messages and the right media to reach them in a compelling way at the right time. It's likely your Eager Beavers are your best, most effective means to engage the Big Middle. That's if you can get them to be your champions inside the company, leveraging their personal engagement in the company mission to connect to their peers among masses in the Big Middle.

Your communications efforts to connect with the Big Middle will be far more successful that way than if you rely exclusively on conventional internal communications tools and messages, and the misnamed "cascade" of information down through the management ranks.

The head of every unit in your company and every facility manager can readily identify their own Eager Beavers. Don't assume they are always going to be managers or supervisors. They exist in all parts of the organization and at all levels. These are the first people you need to reach with critical messages, and then engage them to be your advocates among their peers.

Another common characteristic of this employee type is that they are out-going and friendly. They generally will have developed a high degree of trust among their peers. Naturally, because they stay well informed, they are the ones to whom others turn for news about company changes. Similarly, they are the ones best equipped to knock down false rumors – and they often do just that, without any coaching or urging from their managers to do so.

The Eager Beaver group likely includes a lot of supervisors – I say "likely" because their high degree of engagement means that they are trusted and have probably been promoted. As a rule, supervisors are the most trusted people in an organization, and the primary source of information for most front-line employees. They are also the ones to whom employees confide if there are problems brewing, or if they have ideas to improve operations. Due to this element of trust and Eager Beavers' out-going nature, change messages and breaking news should target them. They immediately understand the rationale and are readily able to digest the change messages and convey them to their colleagues, and then to answer questions that might subsequently arise.

These advocates will respond to the extra attention they're given them and appreciate the recognition. That has the added advantage of assuring that they will become willing messengers. Of course, they are not the sole means of communicating with the Big Middle; they are supplemental. But they just may become the most credible link to the broader employee audience, and a critical means of reinforcing important messages.

Instead of spending the bulk of their time fretting over the nuances of the punctuation of a particular written message, the effectiveness of the latest new communications tool, or the "look" of a new medium, communicators would be far more successful if they focused most of their energies on identifying, cultivating and engaging their internal champions.

Learning Outside Our Comfort Zones

Every business organization hires people for assignments appropriate to their education, background, training, and skills, be it marketers, engineers, designers, accountants, salespeople, or human resource managers.

So is there any value in having people learn specialties outside their own area? Are there benefits for a software company, for example, in having its graphic designers, salespeople, accountants, and marketers learn how to write basic computer code?

The conventional wisdom would say, "No, it would be a waste of time." But one software company CEO felt differently and began to do just that, launching a program to teach every employee JavaScript programming language – just enough so that after a year each would be able to develop a product that could theoretically be integrated into the company's software.

To what end? Certainly not to improve or expand the company's product offering. Why, then?

The CEO of this sixty-employee software firm did it because he felt it "would facilitate more efficiency, bring teams closer together, and ultimately make our company perform better."

This company has since merged with another and changed its name, while the CEO has moved on. Nevertheless, this case provides an instructive operational model. The JavaScript training was not a full-immersion course, intent on creating a back-up engineering team for code writing. Rather, the firm devoted just a few hours each week to lessons, plus lunch-hour "boot camps" led by company engineers. The program started with the expectation that employees would be knowledgeable and moderately proficient after a year.

So did it yield the expected benefits? Apparently so. According to employees interviewed for a follow-up *Boston Globe* article, internal meetings began to take less time because fewer digressive technical explanations were unnecessary. Significant time was saved with shorter internal meetings, which created "found time" for other more productive work related to one's expertise.

One sales executive said that his new coding knowledge enabled him to better explain product attributes to clients instead of having to bring an engineer into some customer meetings for technical explanations and insights.

Left unsaid in the follow-up article was the fact that, instead of bailing out an uninformed salesman, that engineer was able to devote more time to what he did best – what he had been hired for in the first place – a far better investment of his (and the company's) time.

As I read about the result, and as I thought about the broader implications of this effort, the secondary benefits became obvious. For instance, because technology has become such an integral part of our lives, and continues to expand in that regard, it often creates barriers between technical and non-technical people inside companies.

The non-technical side of the population, among which I count myself, knows that having a basic understanding of a relevant technical topic goes far in helping us do our jobs more effectively, especially when we have to interact with technical people or clients.

We also have a better appreciation for the challenges and achievements of our technical colleagues, which helps create a greater sense of empathy and team solidarity. There's an ancillary benefit for the individual employees, as the article pointed out. "At the very least, [employees] realize that knowing JavaScript makes them more marketable. 'It's another resume builder for me,' said the director of accounting operations."

In addition, learning something new as a group, exploring an unknown field together, creates bonds among employees from different parts of the company, thereby building greater camaraderie, morale, and sense of mission.

It also gave employees a new understanding of and greater insights into the company's products, as well as the work and skills that went into their creation and refinement. Imagine the value for marketers, charged with creating and building product awareness among target customers. It wasn't a leap for them to appreciate the full import and market potential of a new product. Similarly, as marketers, it became easier for them to talk with technicians about potential market opportunities that an upgrade or product line extension might yield, opportunities they were sensing in their work because they were more attuned to the nuances of the product.

This needn't be limited to non-technical people learning technical subjects. Why not the other way around, too? Why not teach basic marketing, financial management, or some other aspect of the business to the software engineers?

And we're not just talking about software companies and code writing. No matter the product or service a company sells, there is a technical and/or product research and development side of the business. Helping others in the organization learn the rudiments of the technical side, and vice versa, goes far in breaking down the walls of misunderstanding, ignorance and hostility that often develop in organizations, in turn helping those organizations thrive and grow.

When I started my career fresh out of college as a newspaper reporter, those of us on the editorial side of the curtain were practically fanatical (and a bit arrogant) about remaining ignorant of the advertising sales side of the business – the part of the business, incidentally, that provided our paychecks.

In hindsight, it would have been meaningful and valuable to have a better understanding of and appreciation for the challenges and opportunities that the ad salespeople faced. At the very least, it would have given me new insights into the community I was charged with covering, in which local businesses (our advertisers) played significant roles.

The idea of learning about all the components of a business first-hand is not a new one. It is common in family-owned businesses, for instance, for the children of the founder to work their way up and across the organization. An old friend of mine, now CEO of his sixty-year-old family-owned company, got to his position that way.

Beginning as a teenager working after school and over summer vacations, through high school, college and then after graduation, he worked in virtually every department, including maintenance, manufacturing, sales, customer service, supply chain management, distribution, human resources and, ultimately, marketing, where he attained the position of vice president of marketing by the time he was forty-three.

He eventually succeeded his father as CEO when he was in his mid-fifties and his father stepped aside to become chairman. But consider the broad understanding that my friend had gained of every aspect of his business, which would be impossible for a CEO who had parachuted in from the outside.

Some of the more established large corporations operate similarly, grooming future leaders by exposing them to as many parts of the organization and locations as possible as they climb the corporate ladder. At its very heart, this kind of activity improves internal communications in the organization by helping people better understand and empathize with the various roles and responsibilities of the people who comprise the larger whole.

And any time people with a common mission are better able to understand one another and better equipped to talk on a range of relevant business topics that affect the company, it always accrues to the benefit of the business and, by extension, the bottom line.

"The Glue that Binds Apathy to Vague Strategies"

In mid-2013, the *Wall Street Journal* ran a series of articles about mid-level managers. Full of anecdotes, quotes, and first-hand experiences, the series left me with the distinct impression that being a middle manager has become a pretty tough assignment.

Pushed and pulled in multiple directions, often chasing "stretch" goals under tight deadlines and even tighter budgets, middle managers must keep their bosses happy and subordinates engaged, while ensuring that their business units are contributing effectively toward the company's success, growth and profitability.

The position of middle manager has evolved in parallel with the quickening pace and evolution of business today. Companies must be more responsive to the marketplace and their customers, while sustaining upward revenue and profit curves to satisfy shareholders and owners. These burdens of responsibility fall disproportionately on the shoulders of middle managers, charged with implementing the strategies designed to drive growth.

Yet, making matters still more difficult, many organizations lack clear-cut objectives – or else the objectives change in a seemingly whimsical manner. Sometimes, objectives from different parts of the business work at cross-purposes. In that environment, the approaches that worked last year for a middle manager are irrelevant or ineffective today.

Around the same time as the *Journal* series, Scott Adams, cartoonist and author of the popular "Dilbert" comic, produced a strip one day that succinctly and humorously summed up his view of the current state of affairs for middle managers. The middle manager in this case is the one known as the "Pointy-Haired Boss," who says to his assistant that the CEO has a new strategy, but "it seems vague."

She asks what the engineers will think about it.

He replies, "They don't care about this stuff."

She then asks, "What exactly does a middle manager do?"

And the Pointy-Haired Boss says, "We're the glue that binds apathy to vague objectives."

This assessment may be a cynical view of management at the middle level, but the fact that it makes us laugh reveals its truth. Yes, too often, the CEO's strategy is vague. And, yes, many people within organizations are not singularly focused on the latest strategic edict from on high. But in many cases, it's understandable.

Today, many organizations struggle to build credibility, engagement, and understanding among the employee audience. Often, we've heard employees respond to the latest strategy or initiative with a shrug and an attitude that says, "this too shall pass." They've seen strategic initiatives in the past and all have eventually gone away without effect. So why buy in this time?

The problem with many such strategies is that they often are shaped in a vacuum, apart from the reality of needing to engage managers and employees in their development and implementation. In the end, middle managers are left to digest strategy documents and struggle to make them relevant to their teams.

Senior management in such cases assumes that the organization is following along, when in fact the people are at sea, left to guess their respective roles in effecting the new approach. These shortcomings point up the changing roles and responsibilities in organizations today that must be acknowledged and acted on.

Senior leaders, striving to improve return on investment while assuring that the company has a strong future, must seek to identify and enact the most effective strategy to drive the company in the right direction with a minimum of turmoil or additional cost. Assuring that middle managers and employees are involved in the strategy's development and throughout its implementation goes far in achieving its ultimate success.

Communicators assist leadership in shaping the strategy to assure its alignment with external and internal realities, and then by crafting the appropriate messages to convey the strategy into the organization in a meaningful and relevant way, via the right channels, providing the right context in which to disseminate those messages, at the right cadence. Communicators must also provide the tools and guidance to assure that those messages are relevant across all functions, departments, locations and levels.

Middle managers and supervisors are the people with the most internal credibility among employees and therefore are best positioned to interpret new strategies, adding relevance at the business' front end – i.e., among the very people tasked with producing, marketing, selling, distributing, servicing and supporting the goods and services on which the company and its future success are built.

Middle managers are no longer command-and-control gate-keepers, as in the past, but rather the translators of the challenges and opportunities facing the organization, and the strategies that will guide the organization forward to address them effectively. In other words, their translation of the strategy must make it pertinent and actionable at the unit level.

In summary, a successful future ideally begins with a well-formed strategy, created when the leadership engages the organization and its capabilities, communicated via the middle managers who are provided the context, content, tools and training necessary to engage the people in the future of the organization to understand and proactively perform their respective roles in driving it forward.

Cultivate Your Employees' "Extreme Trust"

In a 2001 feature story about him in *Fortune* magazine, Southwest Airline's founder and former CEO Herb Kelleher said, "You have to treat your employees like customers. When you treat them right, then they will treat your outside customers right. That has been a powerful competitive weapon for us."

I've never forgotten that quote and have used it on many occasions because it cuts to the heart of the purpose of effective employee engagement. Yet it amazes me how many organizations don't follow that guidance, some even going the opposite direction by taking their employees for granted.

A February 2012 article about customer relations in *Fast Company* caught my eye because it provided an apt parallel with respect to the internal environment. "If Your Customers Are Poised for Revolt, It's Time for Extreme Trust" made the case that the transparency and more public environment created by social media has opened up businesses for closer examination by their customers.

No longer can businesses operate in secret, expecting that their customers will follow along in blind loyalty. The author, Don Peppers, explained that, "It used to be that a business could generate substantial profits by keeping its customers in the dark. Entire business models are based on charging customers fees they shouldn't have to pay, or selling them products they don't really need."

Peppers made the case for "extreme trust," which he explained as being "proactively trustworthy, not just by providing a reliable product and competent service, but also by understanding and proactively watching out for your customer's own interest." The case he makes is valid and worthy of consideration by people focusing on their customers. But I contend that the same case can be made for focusing on one's own employees in a parallel fashion, actively seeking to gain their extreme trust.

To help the reader – presumably a businessperson with customers – adjust and respond appropriately by checking her/his own company, Peppers provides a few self-assessment questions. Because I believe that there is a direct connection between employees and customers in the successful business, I've taken most of Peppers' questions and substituted the word "employees" wherever he used the word "customers" – as well as a couple other tweaks so that it makes sense.

See for yourself. How would you answer these questions about your own internal environment and your relationship with your employees?

- Is your company's financial success generally aligned with what's good for your employees?

- Have you identified conflicts between how your firm succeeds, financially, and how it does what's good for your employees, individually?

- Overall, would your company make more money with uninformed, unknowledgeable employees, or from well-informed, knowledgeable ones?

- If an employee is well-informed, knowledgeable, and paying attention, would she/he choose to remain with your company or would she/he be more likely to leave?

- Do your employees proactively prompt one another to avoid errors or oversights? Whether your answer is yes or no: Is this part of their training? Is it part of your company's culture?
- If your business were a government, would your employees be trying to overthrow you?

Last question (my own):

- Are you keeping your employees in the dark, whether deliberately or through your own neglect?

Remember what Herb Kelleher said and take it to heart. If you focus on keeping employees engaged in the business and happy, your customers are the ultimate beneficiaries. And when your customers are happy, they're loyal, which will show up on your bottom line year after year.

That said, go the extra mile by helping employees see the connection between their engagement in the business and customer loyalty. Don't turn it into a routine program with catchy slogans and measurable goals. Rather, make it part of the way your business runs day in and day out.

Left unspoken is the basic underlying reality: that when your employees trust company leadership, their managers and supervisors, when they trust and believe in the common mission, when they see that people at all levels also believe in that mission and demonstrate it in their actions, it will show and be apparent to those who matter the most: the customers.

Deal Directly with Disaffected Employees

When our son was a preschooler, he was plagued by repeated ear infections and persistent colds. Each case meant a trip to the pediatrician for diagnosis and appropriate medication and treatment. After several such instances, his doctor recommended a permanent fix: a tonsillectomy.

So that's what we did. The effect was almost immediate. The ear infections ceased and the frequency of colds dropped to nearly zero. Sure, we could have continued treating the symptoms rather than the cause, but our son wouldn't have been the happy, playful boy he became, nor would he have thrived.

The same is often true in business. Recurring problems can point to deeper issues that are not being diagnosed or addressed. And in the case of recurring efforts by employees to organize for union representation, for instance, the deeper problem often can be traced to poor communications and an insufficient effort to engage employees in the business.

I cite the union organization effort example because a few years ago, a Midwestern manufacturer asked for our advice and counsel in nipping in the bud a surging effort to unionize its assembly line workers. I paid a visit to their headquarters offices along with a colleague who specialized in labor relations and communicating with unionized workers.

We had been provided preliminary background information and insights into the issues and the current situation beforehand. We also did our own research. Among other things, we learned that the threat of union organizing was a recurring headache for this company's management: organizing efforts seemed to pop up every few years. To date, the company had successfully defeated it each instance. This time, however, it seemed more serious and threatening than in the past and the senior management was nervous.

For our meeting with senior managers, we brought a two-part presentation proposing both an immediate solution and a longer-term strategy to stop this situation from recurring.

The two of us sat down with the operations management team, as well as the head of human resources, and the director of corporate communications to hash out the challenge, and to offer our ideas. The managers listened politely and intently to my colleague's recommendations for a near-term approach to dissuade the workforce from voting for union representation. I'd worked with him before and knew his ideas were sound, and had previously proven effective with similar situations.

My part of the presentation came next and centered on a strategic approach to long-term employee communications to gain the trust and understanding of the workforce in the long run, something that clearly was missing in this case. The goal was to assure that workers wouldn't feel the need to organize again in the future by ensuring they knew there was a genuine two-way flow of communications between them and management.

In essence, my part of the proposal called for more frequent contact by senior managers with the hourly workers through a variety of means, including occasional walks through the plant to engage individual employees in conversations, as well as town hall type meetings where they could share relevant information about the state of the business and listen to ideas from the employees. I also recommended an on-going flow of information, through a variety of means, about the external marketplace and its impact on the company to help employees better understand the larger picture.

Though the management team seemed to like our ideas, we left without a commitment and returned home to await their response. They never called back. We later learned that they had somehow headed off the union threat on their own. But a couple years later, I read that the effort to unionize had resurfaced once again.

Why didn't the company management team opt for the more permanent fix of more effective long-term employee engagement? Let me guess. Like a lot of long-term commitments, it demands that you make changes in the way you operate day-to-day. And in the current business climate, that is not a choice a lot of managers like to make. The kind of choices they do like to make are often those that have short-term pay-off: cost cuts that improve margins; changing suppliers for higher quality, greater reliability and/or lower prices; adding staff and production throughput to address increased demand for their products, and the like.

But the kinds of changes we were urging were behavioral, asking managers and company leadership to operate outside their comfort zones and spend more of their limited time out of their offices engaging employees more than they were accustomed to.

It would also have meant they'd have to be more empathetic, and think more about the connections between the employees' world and where the business needed to go.

I'm afraid to say that some managers and leaders seem to take their workforces for granted. The individual employee is brought into the company to perform a specific set of tasks and, in return, is paid a fair wage and benefits. Shouldn't that be enough?

No. It's not enough. Disgruntled employees in dysfunctional organizations engage outside union organizers for their help getting more formal, rigidly controlled engagement with company management on their behalf with union representatives serving as intermediaries to level what they perceive as an uneven playing field.

This appeals to employees who feel cut off from the business anyway and, frankly, have ceased really caring about much beyond the paycheck, the benefits, and a fair and safe work environment – which, of course, is where they believe a union can make a positive difference on their behalf in the absence of an engaged management.

The frustrations that shop floor employees sense when they feel detached from the company's purpose, when their ideas and insights are not sought, when they feel like interchangeable cogs in a machine, are the kinds of aggravations that build up over time, festering to the point where a union organizer finds fertile soil in which to plant the seed for a union shop.

These frustrations and their negative effects can be easily defused with a dose of transparency, honesty, and a healthy two-way flow of information, insights and ideas between employees and management. Unfortunately, this is a lesson that some companies refuse to or seem unable to learn.

When Leaders' Words and Actions are Out of Synch

The higher on the corporate ladder managers are, the more likely it is that people will listen to and heed what they say. That's especially true with the top of the pyramid: the CEO. Not surprisingly, then, when CEOs and other business leaders say one thing but do another, the effect may not match their intent.

I've seen this first-hand myself more than once. But the best example I'm aware of was an experience a friend of mine had with a client company a few years ago. He first met his future client, the head of employee communications for a global management-consulting firm, at a conference.

This chance meeting between my friend, Chris, and his future client, Paul, led to an invitation to meet with him and his communications team to discuss in greater depth the problem the firm was having with an unacceptably high attrition rate among the firm's consultants.

Further, internal surveys had indicated low loyalty scores as well as poor understanding of the firm's mission. Paul said the CEO was blaming poor internal communications. He wanted to get to the bottom of it and reverse the trend.

After an hour-long discussion where Chris and his team offered some preliminary insights, Paul engaged them to do an in-depth assessment and analysis, and to prescribe a solution. Their investigation involved interviews with the CEO and his leadership team, as well as mid-level managers. They also met with several consultants, who comprised the firm's front-line team and chief earning power, as well as the various internal support people.

After the investigative phase, Chris and his team reviewed their findings, compared them to the employee survey results, and began working up prescriptive changes and recommendations. Though there were a number of issues playing into the high attrition rate, the primary problem seemed to the one they had run into most frequently: employees were hearing one thing from leadership but experiencing something else entirely different.

In particular, a recurring theme heard from the CEO was his frequent comment, both verbally and in writing that had become a firm cliché: "We can't be afraid to step on toes." Which Chris learned meant that they must be able to criticize themselves if they were to improve. But, in actual practice, employees told Chris that the opposite was true.

In one example after another, he heard about people that had been honest about issues within the company and how they'd offered ideas to address them. But instead of praise, they had been punished or ostracized by managers and/or leadership. More than once, Chris heard about layoffs that often included the very people that had offered constructive criticism. It had happened too often to be a coincidence, many people said. In other words, leadership said it wanted self-criticism, but really didn't.

In reaction, people initially began to clam up and keep their observations and ideas to themselves. But when that happened, a second result set in: the atmosphere became poisoned.

Problems festered because people were reluctant to step forward to point them out problems or to offer solutions for fear of being "singled out as trouble-makers or complainers," as one young man told Chris.

The final effect was that the internal culture of the organization began to go stale. The better, more talented consultants started looking elsewhere for employment, hence the high attrition rates that were troubling the CEO. He knew he was losing good people, but didn't realize he and his team were the primary reason.

In short, the diagnosis said that the stumbling block was not an employee communications problem but rather one of leadership's words and actions not being in synch. The prescription, then, was not what the CEO was expecting. Chris requested and got a private one-on-one meeting with him to share what he'd learned, playing back some of the comments his own consultants had made about the firm and the leadership.

The CEO was dumbfounded, and initially argumentative. But as Chris provided greater depth in his findings, the CEO soon admitted that he didn't realize he and his team were encouraging criticism while, at the same time, discouraging it.

Fortunately for the firm, he responded assertively, immediately setting about personally to take responsibility for changing things. In the ensuing months, Chris and his team worked with him, his leadership team, and the employee communications unit to re-establish an atmosphere of trust. The effort started small, with the CEO meeting with small groups of employees where he listened, owned up to his inconsistencies, and promised to open lines of communication and provide means to address the organization's shortcomings.

His out-reach efforts were underlined in internal media that spotlighted internal problems and detailed the solutions. Additionally, the media subsequently provided periodic progress updates, while saluting the consultants that had stepped forward with solutions. Over time, the CEO did improve internal trust. But it

115

was time-consuming. Nevertheless, to his credit, he realized how critical it was to the future health and well being of the company, so he made it a priority and, by example, made sure his leadership team did too.

Chris had told me about the investigative and prescriptive phases, but I'd not heard how it turned out in the long run. Checking back with Paul a couple years later, Chris was pleased to report that the firm's attrition rates had fallen and employee loyalty scores had risen. He said he later got a note from the CEO thanking his team for their work, acknowledging the positive effect their change in attitude and approach had had.

But Chris said the most gratifying sentence in that note were the closing words: "I have come to realize that the example we set as leaders with our actions is far more important and impactful than any words we can ever say, no matter how clever or heart-felt they may be."

Establish Trust in Your First Days on the Job

Their first days on the job are their best opportunity for managers new to their jobs to connect with their teams, and to establish a level of rapport, trust and cooperation that will likely spell the difference between long-term success and near-term failure in their new positions. Old-fashioned face-to-face engagement and communication are the keys, especially the listening component.

However, many new managers' initial focus is almost exclusively on their new boss and the expectations that come with the job. Naturally, we want to please the person who hired us, and has the power to promote us – or fire us. But neglecting the people who report to us can have a long-term impact from which no boss, no matter how much she/he may like you and your work, can save you.

A friend of mine was on the receiving end of a manager like this. He had been at his job for a couple years when his unit manager left for a new opportunity, and a new manager came aboard to take over.

Other than introducing himself, this new guy, "John," didn't bother to interview his 14 new direct reports. He never showed much interest in them, nor did he ask them about their outside interests, their desires, their backgrounds or experience. Frankly, John never seemed to think of or treat them as individuals with unique skills. On the other hand, as the months and years passed, John seemed always to focus on the new people that he had personally recruited to the company as the operation grew. As time went on, he showed himself

117

to be closer to them, going out of his way to compliment their work, amidst his silence toward the people on his team he had inherited, those who had more seniority with the company than he.

My friend says that he never trusted John, nor did he believe much of what he said. He cautiously weighed whatever John told him and his peers, and privately second-guessed nearly every directive from him. Can't say I blame him. Would you care to work for someone like John?

With that in mind, here are a few ideas for what we need to address in our first days as a new manager if we want to avoid being like John, to ensure long-term employment, as well making valuable contributions to the organization and its success.

Yes, of course we should connect with our new boss to delineate the job parameters, performance metrics and his/her expectations of us. If appropriate, we should also meet with other managers with whom we will be working, or to whom we may have dotted line reporting relationships, to get an understanding of their expectations and how they operate.

We must also get a clear understanding of the organization's mission, vision and values, and specifically our unit and/or division's role in that regard. What are the key drivers of success? How will success be measured? What are the chief challenges and opportunities facing the company and our unit? Are there any near- or long-term strategies and initiatives that we need to be aware of? What's the competitive environment? What challenges are our customers facing?

Concurrently with this early investigation, and just as important, we must also begin connecting individually with our direct reports. As soon as we get settled into our new office space, if not sooner, we should be setting up appointments to spend some meaningful face-to-face time with these people. By "meaningful," I don't mean that should just make small talk with them. Allow enough time to find out more about them personally and professionally, listening and learning by asking about:

- Their backgrounds (education, previous employment, etc.).
- How long they've been employed there.
- What attracted them to the company in the first place.
- If they are fairly new hires, whether their initial expectations have been met.
- If they are long-time employees, how the company has evolved – for better and/or worse – during their tenure.
- Their roles, both assigned and assumed.
- Current issues they are facing.
- The challenges and opportunities facing the unit itself and how they think the team should approach them.
- Their expectations of me, their new manager.
- What kind of support and resources I can help provide them that will help make them more effective in their jobs.
- Their personal and professional goals.
- Whether they see an obvious track for their future inside the company, and whether the company has supported those goals.
- Whether they've gotten the training and support they felt they've needed, and if not, why not.

Where appropriate, share your own relevant personal stories to illustrate and expand on your questions.

Without asking directly, try to sense any frustrations they might be feeling on the job, such as whether they have felt stifled in any way or made to feel that they've gone as far they can in the organization. Also, without asking directly, try to discern whether any personal or family issues might interfere with their work and, if so, how the company has helped (or not), and if there's anything you as their manager can do for them in that regard.

That said, I'd like to add a personal admonishment. If your inquiry elicits any negative comments about the company in general or any other managers in particular, keep the comments between you and the other person. Don't betray their confidence by sharing their concerns with your manager or anyone else in the company – even if you think you're being helpful. It happened to me once, and I never trusted that boss again.

You shouldn't expect to come away from all these interviews with answers to all these questions, or a complete picture of all your direct reports. Some people are naturally reticent to open up to a new manager. That's okay. What counts is the spirit of the effort, the attempt you've made to show that you care. Just showing your interest in such matters goes a long way in the process of building trust and empathy, the kind of trust you will need to be effective in your job as a manager and team leader. And, you have opened the door for future conversations, as they grow more comfortable with you as their manager.

The important thing at this stage is to ask the questions, to demonstrate your interest in your team members as human beings, and as individual contributors. You will get to know them better once you've begun working with them on a day-to-day basis. And you will soon find out who your most valuable team members are. That early demonstration of trust will help assure that you are all on the same team, working toward common goals.

Getting Through Our Hitting Slumps

"The greatest manager has a knack for making players think they are better than they think they are." – Reggie Jackson

One evening, I was watching a Red Sox baseball game on television. As a batter stepped to the plate, the announcer, Don Orsillo, noted that the player was in the middle of a long hitting slump, having gone hitless for some 15 games.

Orsillo asked Steve Lyons, the color commentator, whether players in that situation get demoralized and spiral even further into a funk. Lyons had played nearly 20 years in the Major Leagues for the Red Sox and three other teams. So his answer was insightful and instructive.

"If you're in a hitting slump like that," he said, "you go to the ballpark the next day fully confident that you're going to go four-for-four. Nobody in that situation goes to the game expecting to extend the hitless streak." And here was Lyon's most telling comment: "You are not in the Major League if that's your attitude. And you will not make it in the big leagues if you don't have tons of confidence."

My first reaction was his insight's application to my own attitude. In fact, that kind of thinking is applicable in how people operate as business managers and leaders. Clearly the more successful people in business – the ones playing in the "majors" – are those that can walk away from defeats and see them as learning experiences, who can start each new day fully confident that that day they will go four-for-four.

By extension, people that become leaders will guide their companies to success if they are able to imbue their people and their organizations with the same attitude, resurrecting and sustaining confidence after defeat, always moving forward with self-assurance.

Yes, it's tough to do that. And the leader who is able to consistently buck up his/her team's confidence through trials and after stinging defeats is respected and, more importantly, heeded whenever times get tough. Communicating certainty like that isn't so much as just words and speeches as it is leading by example.

For instance, it is instructive to watch how General Motors' CEO, Mary Barra, addressed her company's challenges around massive vehicle recalls for faulty ignitions in her first months on the job. Clearly those recalls represented failures and mistakes at several levels of the organization, failures and mistakes that were repeated.

The task before Ms. Barra was to right the ship and get GM back into a winning formula of developing, manufacturing and marketing high quality vehicles that people want to own. To do that, she had to encourage her people to learn from their mistakes and move on. She had to remind them that it was its people that once made GM great. She had to convince them that that excellence still resides within them, and to move forward with confidence as a unified whole.

Her employees had to see Ms. Barra herself consistently operating with confidence herself, demonstrating through her own actions the central role of excellence and quality. All the while that central tenet had to be echoed in her spoken and written words.

In the end, years from now, she will be judged on how quickly and how completely she turned around the ocean liner known as General Motors. It is no small task, to be sure. So if she is judged successful in the end, if GM resumes its role as the world's leading auto company under her guidance, she will go down as one of GM's greatest leaders. And it will be because she led her organization with confidence.

Leadership excellence, in that regard, is not just for those who must right a foundering ship like GM. It is also seen in leaders able to sustain excellence and a reputation for innovation. In that respect, the jury is still out – and getting impatient – with Tim Cook, Apple's CEO who inherited the venerable cloak of excellence and innovation from the late Steve Jobs.

At the annual Worldwide Developers' Conference in San Francisco every June, Jobs would habitually thrill Apple fans with groundbreaking new products: iPod, iPhone, iPad, etc. Since Jobs' death in October 2011, when Cook took over as CEO, there have been few such groundbreaking products. Rather, Cook and his team have mostly improved existing products and expanded established lines.

The fact that the Apple Watch was not immediately perceived as another one of those breakthrough products on the order of the iPad, iPhone and iPod tells us that Cook lacks the Jobs magic. And what was that magic? It was Jobs' infectious confidence and commitment to excellence in everything that Apple put its name on. While I have great respect for Cook's management abilities and operational excellence, I've never sensed the same charisma or magnetic enthusiasm that Jobs demonstrated consistently. Jobs was a visionary. People of his ilk come along very rarely.

As outsiders, we cannot know how well Cook has filled Jobs' leadership shoes in the CEO role. Nor do we know how well he has established himself as an inspirational leader. But that tenure should be long enough for anyone to do so, and from outward appearances, it isn't clear that Cook has succeeded. Oh yes, Apple is still thriving and is still highly valued, with the highest market capitalization of any company. It still makes great products. And yes, that's likely because Cook is one of the best operational leaders in the business – the reason Jobs hired him in the first place and the reason he was promoted. But the competition – especially Samsung and Google – has caught up with and, in some cases, surpassed Apple's innovation.

Has Cook instilled the kind of confidence in his people that Jobs once did? The genius of Steve Jobs lay not only in his innovative vision, but also his ability to convince people they were better than they thought they were. Jobs was the kind of guy who would go to the plate in the midst of a hitting slump and know – just know – that his next swing of the bat would produce a home run. Jobs was supremely and contagiously confident. Can the same be said of Tim Cook? I don't see the evidence.

Actions Speak Louder...

Humor works best when it contains a grain of truth – which is probably why I got such a hearty laugh from one particular "Dilbert" cartoon. In it, the "Pointy-Haired Boss" enters Dilbert's cubicle, coffee mug in hand, saying, "I'm here to be your role model. My actions speak louder than my words. Just drink them in." This elicits a blank stare from Dilbert. The boss then says, "I think you're doing your part wrong."

Yes, the Pointy-Haired Boss is an extreme and farcical version of the clueless manager, the kind of a manager who peruses the latest best-selling business book for new ideas, while ignoring all that goes on around him.

We might infer that he had read that the best, most important communications are demonstrated through actions rather than what he says – which is true. We've all known people like this – though I hope, for your sake, that your boss isn't like him. He stands there and claims to be a role model his employees should emulate – or at least admire – all the while wondering why it isn't so.

He reminds me of the Michael Scott character in NBC's "The Office" or, better still, Bill Lumbergh in the movie, "Office Space." Both are managers in title alone. Lumbergh ostentatiously parks his Porsche 911 in his reserved parking space right by the front door of the "Initech" offices, as though to inspire his employees to aspire to the same for themselves. He presents himself with a false aura of concern when, in fact he has none, is incapable of empathy, and, in the course of the film, is singularly and ruthlessly focused on cutting his department's payroll.

Michael Scott, on the other hand, is the kind of boss who thinks his weird sense of humor endears him to his staff – when the opposite is true. He is blind to his oafishness and lack of genuine empathy for his employees.

Just because Bill Lumbergh, Michael Scott and the Pointy-Haired Boss have been elevated to management positions, they conclude that they have a license to be thickheaded bores, out of touch with the daily struggles and challenges their employees face. They are full of false swagger derived from their sense that a job title alone bestows upon them unique vision and wisdom.

Unfortunately, in many places, that's true. People are elevated up the management ladder for a number of reasons, but not always the right ones. It's the "Peter Principle" in action: "Every employee tends to rise to his level of incompetence."

So the Pointy-Haired Boss probably read his new management book and concluded that his employees need to pay more attention to his non-verbal cues since, he imagines, he's such an amazing guy with so many talents that should be emulated. But he skipped the lessons about engaging them in the first place; the ones that help give them reasons to trust him. Instead, he fixated on his desired end result of reverential and attentive employees.

The other truth embedded in the cartoon is that the employee has a role in communications. And that is true, too. Organizations that cultivate that by encouraging two-way communications are far more likely to be successful in the long run than the business that sees communications as a one-way, top-down affair.

In fact, communication and engagement is an in-the-trenches kind of thing. The boss that is the best role model is the one who models the behaviors she/he expects to get from employees. They never tell their people what they want them to do and be. Rather, they demonstrate it through their own actions, and thereby establish an atmosphere of trust and mutual respect. Consider the following examples.

In early 2014, Don Knauss, CEO of Clorox Company, spoke to the *New York Times* for its Sunday "Corner Office" feature. He said his background as a commissioned U.S. Marine Corps lieutenant gave him lasting lessons in how best to manage his employees.

"It's all about your people," he said. "If you're going to engage the best and the brightest and retain them, they'd better think that you care more about them than you care about yourself. They're not about making you look good. You're about making them successful. If you really believe that and act on that, it gains you credibility and trust. You can run an organization based on fear for a short time. But trust is a much more powerful, long-term and sustainable way to drive an organization."

Former Southwest Airlines CEO Herb Kelleher never hesitated to pitch in to load baggage on and off planes when he saw that a crew was short-handed or the plane was delayed because of it. He also helped out at the gate check-in, if he happened to be in the airport and saw that the lines were getting too long. Imagine the trust and respect he earned among his employees.

At a client company, I once met a factory manager who went out of his way to pass through the plant at least twice a day, walking to and from the parking lot in the morning and evening. Every day he was on site, he left himself enough time to stop and chat with his line workers. Over time, he came to understand deeply, and on a personal level, the challenges his employees faced, as well as their insights and ideas for achieving greater productivity. The fact that he enacted many of their ideas built a level of trust with them that had not existed before.

I heard a story second-hand about the general manager of a luxury hotel who, in his first six months on the job, worked in every department of the operation and came to understand the many daily challenges that his employees faced in assuring customers' stays were pleasant and enjoyable experiences. In putting himself in their shoes, literally, he developed genuine respect, understanding and empathy for his employees. He could talk with them intelligently about their jobs and solicit their ideas for making the hotel a better, more welcoming place for their guests.

There are many other such examples, undoubtedly, but the common thread throughout is that these managers and leaders made it central to their jobs to learn as much as they could about their operations and employees, to connect with the world of their employees, and attain a genuine empathy for them as a path to getting the best performance out of them. These people see themselves as part of the larger team, not above it or apart from it.

Employees emulate their managers and leaders when they feel there is a genuine sense of interest in them. As a result, they come to trust those leaders and see them as authentic role models.

IV. Effective Employee Communications

IV. Effective Employee Communications

*"The ability to express an idea is…
as important as the idea itself."*

Bernard Baruch

Question, Listen, Discuss and Debate

"The communication continuum" is a shorthand way of referring to the back-and-forth exchange of information and ideas between and among managers, leaders and employees through various means. In the ideal case, the manager is questioning and listening as much as or more than speaking and conveying information.

But if listening and seeking input is so important, why do so many managers fall short in that department?

I suspect the short answer has to do with finite time: managers have much to accomplish and not enough time in which to do it. So in the communication continuum, it often feels more critical for them just to disseminate information and data to their teams, and then move onto the next task, phone call, or meeting.

Certainly there are times in the typical workweek when that is necessary. But the manager that falls into the habit of blaming a hectic workweek for overusing top-down, one-way communication is on track for failure down the road.

In this era of Twitter, Facebook, email, and text messages, we have become accustomed to taking the easy route when communicating with our teams. A mass email to all team members alerting them to a change of process or policy is certainly appropriate.

But when email blasts become managers' principal (or only) means of communicating to their teams, then they are no longer communicating. They are spewing. Such information dumps fall on deaf ears and unseeing eyes. Let's remember that the reason we build teams of people within our organizations is to achieve the excellence that several people working together can attain that the individual working alone cannot. So it stands to reason that people managing that team want to tap into the best that their players bring to the mix.

Questioning, listening and engaging in proactive dialogues are how the best managers do that. So what exactly does that look like, ideally? Again, I add the word "ideally" because we have to be cognizant that the push-and-pull of day-to-day business can sometimes overwhelm and cancel out the good intentions of striving for excellent communication.

So let's assume that the periodic ebb and flow of busy-ness on the job allows for contemplative moments when one-on-one conversations or productive team meetings can occur. The well-organized manager knows best when those times are most likely to be available – first thing Monday mornings; at the end of the billing cycle; before the next production run gets started; after the quarterly reports are finished, etc.

The wise manager with foresight finds those periodic opportunities and works them into everyone's calendar. Those times become the most valuable of the workweek (or month). When the manager and team members are prepared, much can be accomplished, and the ball figuratively moved down the field.

Please note that preparation on both sides is critical but means something a bit different, though it follows parallel tracks. In addition to coming to these periodic meetings prepared with the right information and all the necessary background details, the manager should bring an open mind, ready to listen and learn things he may not expect, as well as a desire to discover and discern specific information related to issues of the moment, in particular the current challenges and opportunities the team is dealing with.

A significant component of managers' preparations require staying plugged into the larger organization and the outside world that impacts the business as a whole. They should be able to bring that information to their teams and make it relevant to their day-to-day efforts.

These meetings are also chances to reflect together on how their unit might work better with other units, how collectively they can contribute to the organization's larger purpose. To that end, it is the manager's responsibility to bring in the outside view that is not regularly conveyed into the confines of a unit's figurative four walls.

For their part, the employees' responsibility is to come to these discussions with ideas, insights and open minds. Their preparation is best achieved over the course of doing their jobs, making note of problems that recur, and recommended solutions, as well as opportunities that they sense are not being fully exploited.

These are the gems that alert managers with good listening skills look for and hope for. At the same time, managers encourage the sharing of bad news along with the good because they know that responding negatively to the employee who brings the bad news will only discourage others from doing so in the future, which in turn leads to small problems being ignored, and then festering into intractable crises.

I fear that the typical team meeting consists of a manager speaking for a short time, concluding his/her remarks and then asking whether anyone has any questions. Hearing none, everyone returns to work. The result is that employees often feel purposeless and a mere cog in a machine, disconnected from the larger operation.

It is far more effective to allow the team to learn together with the manager posing open-ended questions that force them to think through a challenge or opportunity and arrive at their own answers. They then share those answers with the team and begin a discussion and debate.

Together, the team learns while often coming up with realistic solutions, or uncovering new ways of looking at and thinking about challenges and opportunities. At the same time, the individual employee becomes more engaged in the business, feeling she/he is an active contributor to its larger purpose, and that their voice is heard. It's all good. It's effective communications.

Communicating Corporate Values, or *Tchotchkes*?

One day, a seemingly innocuous question on a Linked In forum about employee communications stirred responses that befuddled me.

An Indonesian woman working for a company in Djakarta posed the original question. She asked, "Please advise a nice and quite simple souvenir for employees to promote company values." I was late to the discussion. It had already wallowed in the relative merits of mouse pads versus coffee mugs and the like on which to print the company's values. The advice seemed to center on how much to spend and picking the sort of gift that people would want to keep, preferably on their desks.

Oh dear.

Fortunately, it wasn't all like that. Further down in the discussion chain, I found one fellow from Chicago who wrote the following:

> *"My emphatic answer: None of the above, and nothing of the sort you are asking for. The best way to reinforce values is to train and reward senior managers for the consistent, visible exhibition of behaviors, comments, and decisions that affirm and endorse those values. Focus your attention at the top level, and devote a considerable amount of effort to ensuring that front-line supervisors do the same. Skip the quizzes and the coffee mugs and lapel pins and laminated cards. Just work relentlessly on visibly modeling the values from day to day."*

"Bravo!" I thought. Heartened by that counsel, I contributed my own two cents, echoing and endorsing that view by adding the following:

> *"If you want to trivialize the importance of a company's values, put them on a poster, coffee mug, or mouse pad. On the other hand, if your goal is to reinforce the values that drive the company toward success ... reward the right behaviors of your supervisors and your middle and senior managers. When their daily words and actions, and their interactions with their direct reports echo the intent and spirit of the company's values, it's far more likely that your organization will be performing its best for the long-term. Giving out trinkets and such is just a waste of time and money."*

I was pleased to see a couple of other participants endorse our view. But nevertheless, the silly responses kept coming. There was little debate, just the continuing admonitions to avoid giving employees cheap gifts that get thrown away, favoring this or that alternative.

I don't want to make assumptions or cast aspersions at businesspeople in emerging economies like Indonesia and conclude that this young woman in her naïveté about cultivating corporate values is typical of that country's business practices. That wouldn't be fair, particularly in light of the fact that comments that encouraged her to tie her company's values to *tchotchkes* and gewgaws came from people who work for organizations in the developed world in places like the U.S., U.K., Australia and Israel. An American respondent offered as his idea "a values-imprinted water bottle."

Could someone possibly tell me what the link might be between a water bottle and the values printed on it? Are we to expect that every time an employee takes a drink from that water bottle, she/he will pause and reflect on the corporate values? Not likely. A company's values are its touchstones. They may be best conveyed with words, but they are not merely words on paper (or water bottles or mouse pads).

In fact and in practice, values should embody the core truths of the organization as they are lived day in and day out by its leaders and founders. As the word implies, what behaviors does the business <u>value</u>? What behaviors do leaders and managers encourage and reinforce through reward and recognition? Once a business is established and profitable enough to hire employees, its values should also be apparent. They are the uncompromising beliefs that are recognized and rewarded to reinforce the desired actions that drive the organization forward toward its vision.

Typically, values encompass integrity or honesty, quality, and customer focus – words to that effect. They would also include relevant characteristics that underline and support the company's chosen field. For instance, a value for a restaurant would likely include cleanliness, while entrepreneurial spirit is an important value for a small start-up.

So, to the intent of the woman's original question, how do you cultivate values, particularly in a large, established business?

Pull the company's leadership together to put into words the behaviors that they value, as succinctly as possible. They should reach consensus on those words. Then, they should talk about the values among their teams. And there's nothing wrong with reinforcing that by including them as part of the corporate profile.

But, as my fellow correspondent from Chicago said, you're going to achieve the desired behaviors far more effectively by living the values and working *"relentlessly on visibly modeling the values from day to day"* than by wasting your money on useless gifts.

A Four-Star General's View of Communications

In the context of mortal combat, far from home base with all hell breaking loose, there is nothing more critical than good communications. Well, that and lots of ammunition, along with air and artillery support. But even so, without reliable, consistent communications, you will never have enough ammo.

The parallel in business is that you may be able to throw a lot of money and people at challenges or crises, but without effective communications, it won't make a lot of difference. That's why the words of wisdom from retired four-star General Stanley McChrystal ring so true, in a terrific interview that appeared in *Inc.* magazine in early 2012.

Gen. McChrystal was commander of the Joint Special Operations Command (JSOC) in Afghanistan during its peak period of engagement from 2003 to 2006. He is also a third-generation West Point graduate – a soldier's soldier, as the expression goes. My naïve image of such a man is one of rigid hierarchy, someone who lives and breathes "chain of command," with little patience for the softer part of operations – i.e., the people side of the equation. So I was pleasantly surprised to read in this brief interview his strong belief in the importance in building relationships with direct reports as a precursor to establishing effective communications before crises hit.

He talked about the value of the physical communications links – telephones and the Internet, for instance – but said that relationships are most important, which he explains as "having people you know and trust that you can communicate effectively with so you can get a clear understanding of the situation and you can begin to craft a credible response."

In other words, the cultivation and maintenance of relationships are the keys to effective communications, which in turn is central to being able to successfully respond to the challenges everyone faces, in both war and everyday business – which are often inconvenient and unanticipated. Not only is it unwise to await crises to begin the effort to build relationships and establish firm communications links. But, also, to wait is to guarantee failure.

Especially in the context of a crisis – whether it's on the battlefield or in the office – the lack of a foundation of established relationships and the trust they embody means that communications will be chaotic and largely worthless. A guiding vision or mission is the single most effective way to build those relationships in an organization, to unite people around a shared sense of purpose, everyone striving for the same ultimate result. The same is true in a military context.

Gen. McChrystal shares that philosophy, though he uses a different term. "We develop something called 'commander's intent' to put in clear words what it is we really mean ... designed to explain, in the commander's own voice, what it is we were going to do, why we thought that was important, how it fit in to the bigger context of what we were trying to do, and then what might be successful."

I've rarely read a better, more succinct description and purpose of "vision" than that.

As though reading my mind, he went on to say that, in business, "commander's intent ... might be 'vision'... It would explain to people, here's what we're trying to do, and if things aren't exactly as you expected them to be, this is still the end result. If you empower each employee with that kind of context and under-standing, they get what we call 'shared consciousness and purpose.' They suddenly understand what it is they are trying to do in what environment, and what the organization is trying to accomplish."

Beautifully said. People within a business who fully understand and work toward a vision will always encounter stumbles and barriers along the way. The strategy they so carefully worked out may not unfold exactly as they had planned. But they still keep their eyes on the desired end results, as laid out in the vision.

There's an old expression about war strategy and planning: that as soon as the fighting breaks out, the first thing to get tossed aside is the plan. Chaos rules, but the end goal remains unchanged. When people work toward a common vision, the way they communicate and the words they use come more naturally. There is less guessing as to another person's meaning and intent since they all know where they're going and their communications are built on the trust inherent in established relationships.

In a military context, say in Afghanistan, if the commanding general's intent is secure the Helmand province for the local citizens desirous of peace, then the strategy and component tactics toward that end make sense. The officers within the chain of command continually reemphasize that desired end result, making it relevant for better understanding among their troops.

As they then move as a unit, securing the province by battling back the local Taliban forces, in the face of chaos and mayhem of battle, their plans change on the fly.

And at the most basic level – be it the platoon or even the squad – the subtle communications occur between corporals and their men, or between a sergeant and the members of his platoon by means of a mix of hand signals and brief voice commands that speak volumes, built on established relationships of mutual trust and understanding. We face our own virtual Taliban every day in business – albeit, not mortally dangerous.

When we're able to stay focused on the vision that drives our organization, we're able to communicate our intentions clearly to our teammates to surmount the daily struggles and setbacks, better able to help meet the ultimate goals of the organization.

Virtual Communications for Virtual Employees

The time we spend working during our productive years represent the bulk of our waking hours. Consequently, the people we work with often become good friends and the people we know the best.

This was especially so in the traditional nine-to-five, Monday-through-Friday office routine that – along with lifetime employment that was prevalent in the post-World War Two years in America – is now largely a thing of the past. While it lasted, it helped establish numerous deeply embedded corporate cultures based on the relationships that people developed working side-by-side, day-in and day-out.

That's all changed. Slowly, at first, technological advances made it possible to work away from the office. First came the fax machine and FedEx overnight delivery of important documents. The speed of change ratcheted up considerably in the past ten to fifteen years with the advent and then widespread adoption of the Internet by businesses and its penetration into so much of what we do.

By the way, it was only 1999 that GE's former CEO Jack Welch "discovered" the Internet and urged his peers to do likewise or risk being left behind. And don't forget that Microsoft was late to the party with its Internet Explorer web browser, well after Netscape was the default Internet browser.

The Internet and its myriad technologies, the hardware and software, have now enabled us to be effective workers no matter where we are. First, it was email. More recently it's Skype, iChat, and web services like GoToMeeting where people can work together in real time no matter where they are. Twenty or thirty years ago, working from home one or two days a week – if not all the time – would have been unthinkable. Today, it's what we're used to it. In fact, working from home a couple days a week is often considered a perquisite of the job.

But paralleling that evolution, we've seen the deconstruction of the conventional office routine, where your boss is down the hall in the corner office. I recently consulted for a large multinational firm with its headquarters in Boston. The person in charge of North American sales – a senior vice president and a member of the senior management team – worked out of his home in Boulder, CO.

I asked him whether it impeded his ability to be an effective manager. "Not at all," he said. "I'm on the road most of the time anyway, so it really doesn't matter where I set up my office. If I'm needed at headquarters, I can be there tomorrow morning."

A friend of mine works for an international conglomerate. Due to increased state corporate and personal income taxes in Massachusetts, the company recently relocated much of its operations across the border to New Hampshire.

He had been accustomed to a half-hour commute by train into downtown Boston, but the relocation expanded his commute to more than sixty miles by car – each way. He told me he now works from home three days a week and spends twelve to fourteen hours a day in the office the other two days.

The jarring aspect of this new arrangement, he said, is the radical change it has imposed on his unit's unique culture. The office space where the transferred employees now work is vacant of much of the staff most of the time, he said. The camaraderie that he had known for years is now gone. He rarely sees his colleagues face-to-face any more – though they do converse on the phone regularly. But it's not the same thing.

Assuming this is now the norm, we can infer the dispersion of employees from central offices will continue and their numbers will increase. What effect does this new paradigm have on employee communications and one's ability to manage people effectively?

In a nutshell, it means managers and leaders have to work even harder to establish and sustain solid communication links with their employees. Certainly the best communication is face-to-face. We can assume that the manager-employee relationship is initially established with a face-to-face meeting, supplemented with periodic personal visits. But over the long term, it behooves managers to maintain those critical relationships with a regular flow of two-way information through any and all possible and practical means: email, text messages, telephone, voice mails, Intranet chat rooms, and every other tried-and-true method that works in a given organization.

I hasten to add that, as noted in "Employee Engagement is a Two-Way Street" (page 90), the employee him or herself bears an equal burden to assure that the lines of communication remain open. If you don't hear from your boss when you expect to, don't take it as a personal affront. He/she is likely very busy. Pick up the phone.

Sure, you may miss the opportunities to participate in office betting pools on the Super Bowl or NCAA's "March Madness." And you may miss the chance encounters at the water cooler to catch up on personal news with your employees, and to see photos of their kids growing up. Unfortunately, these aspects of our work lives that add depth to our friendships are being lost to the surge of technology and the push for greater efficiencies. But we can't afford to let it also sacrifice the effective working relationships and communications that drive the business and its success.

How Business is like Baseball

A sportswriter once characterized baseball as a game of "suddenness – suddenly, anything can happen." But what a range of possible happenings the game presents. While it's a game of subtleties, if you know baseball well and know what to watch for, you generally have a pretty good idea of what might happen next. Even then, the range of possibilities is virtually numberless. But at least you know in general what to expect.

It's all there in front of you and it's only a matter of being familiar enough with the nuances of the game and the two particular teams on the field to be able to assess the situation and make a fair prediction about what might or should happen next.

The circumstances at any given point in the game and their variations are infinite. The most skillful ballplayers and fans know how each particular set of circumstances should be played, both offensively and defensively: whether the infielders and/or outfielders should play shallow or deep; what kind of pitch the catcher should call for; whether the batter should swing for the fences, bunt, or "take" the next pitch (not swing); whether the runner on first base should take a short lead to keep the pitcher honest, or attempt to steal second. And on and on it goes.

The same holds true with business. There are an infinite number of possibilities for each given situation. But unlike the game of baseball played on a finite field that's completely in view, you can't always readily perceive all the variables that can come into play in a given business situation. For instance, in a weak and uncertain economy, should your company invest in new plants, equipment and people, or hoard your cash in a protective crouch?

The answer, of course, depends on a number of factors, not the least of which is your company's position in its industry versus your competitors; the strength of your new product development pipeline; the relative strength or weakness of the markets and customers to whom you sell your products/services; and your cash flow and cash reserve, to name just a handful of variables.

That's why it's imperative for all people, no matter their position or level of responsibility within your organization, to be fully cognizant at all times of all that impacts the business. That includes the dynamics both inside and, especially, outside the company. Think of the business arena as a ball field, with a lot of different players, each with different roles and capabilities.

The trouble is that business is not as simple as a baseball game with just two competing teams on the field. It's more like a free-for-all paintball tournament without teams. It's you against everyone else. While you take aim at one player in front of you, you've failed to notice the opponent lurking behind an adjacent tree about to fire a pellet at your backside and take you out of the game.

This is where effective internal communications come in. Communications are central in helping a business achieve success, repeatedly and well into the future.

A smoothly operating communications function is a company's best means of assuring that its people stay well informed about the evolving paradigm in which the company operates, such as new competitive threats, evolving and expanding governmental regulations, increased corporate taxes, or the hurricane that's bearing down on your largest manufacturing plant on the Gulf Coast.

At the same time, communications must provide the means by which those same people can communicate up and down and across the organization to share insights and ideas, while seeking answers to their unique challenges.

In short, the communications function and the people who manage it must operate as though they were the play-by-play announcer sitting in the broadcast booth high above home plate. He brings to bear his wisdom from years of playing and watching the game, combined with his eye for the action and the added advantage of having the best seat in the house.

Even still, it's an imperfect analogy because it's more than that. It's as though while you're calling the game for the fans listening on the radio, you're also facilitating the means by which the fans can tune into your broadcast and ask questions about a particular play, or offer an insight about the game. In short, it's a tough assignment, and a very important one.

Economic Realities in the Workplace

As mentioned a couple other places in this book (especially the previous entry), the importance of bringing knowledge and awareness of the outside world into organizations cannot be overemphasized. The stubbornly sluggish economy we've been experiencing for the past several years has put a variety of strains on business, adding new imperatives in this regard.

Companies struggle to maintain profitability (or even stay in business) amid feeble market conditions, never mind trying to grow. Meanwhile, it's difficult for their employees to be at their best when they worry about the potential loss of their jobs (or those of their co-workers). This particular period is all the more difficult for businesses because of the added burdens and uncertainties spawned largely in the political arena around issues like:

- The ever-present possibility of increases in business, property, and personal income taxes at federal, state, and local levels.
- The growth of federal, state, and local regulations and red tape.
- Federal, state, and local minimum wage increases.
- The rising cost of healthcare insurance combined with the imposition of the Affordable Care Act that brings with it a plethora of new regulations, costs and taxes.
- Energy policy changes (various efforts to "regulate carbon emissions" and/or reduce the use of fossil fuels) that result in increased costs for energy – a big line item for any company.

Individually and collectively, these add to the cost, complexity and challenge of doing business, both today and in the future, putting further constraints on businesses' ability to focus on what they do best and to expand by hiring and retaining qualified people, buying modern equipment, and building new facilities.

As Congress, state legislatures and other political leaders debate whether to increase taxes and/or to impose new regulations, business leaders and owners hesitate, paralyzed by the uncertainties of additional costs and controls implicit in many of the proposals that could arise in the coming months and years.

They know it's dangerous to make commitments that will increase their costs, liquidity they may not have a year from now. That translates into postponement of hiring new people – since additional employees represent long-term investments – or incurring debt to build plants that may not run at capacity in a weak economy.

Instead, businesses hoard cash against the possibility that they will have to spend it later on things like elevated taxes, higher energy costs and/or increased healthcare premiums. And some politicians have the gall to criticize them for their caution, accusing them of "hoarding" their cash as though to do so is a crime.

Unfortunately, some employees are divorced from these external economic realities. Within many companies, certain myths tend to persist: that the company is virtually immune to natural economic forces; that it has infinitely deep pockets with which to pay ever-rising wages and benefits; that company management is over-stating the impact of external forces on the business; that company leadership is over-compensated; and that they can always raise prices to maintain profitability.

Though tempting, the answer does not lie in passing along increased costs in the form of higher prices. While some price increases might be possible, this route is never the only solution. Besides, customers can likely find less expensive sources, postpone their purchases, or do without altogether, depending on the product or service. Employees, no matter their role within the company, need to have a solid understanding of things like revenues, cash flow, and profits in the context of rising costs.

Employees must appreciate that increased expenses – whether in the form of taxes, energy costs or healthcare premiums – impede the company's ability to earn a profit, and that profits ensure that an organization can continue to operate well into the future.

Put another way, a business' future is contingent on whether it can update plants and equipment, maintain those plants and that equipment, recruit new talent, and improve and update its employees' talents and skills – all of which are impossible in the absence of profits. A stagnant organization – one unable to reinvest in itself and its people – is an organization in its early death throes.

Those harsh economic realities and the uncertainties of our times must be part of the ongoing internal dialogue. In truth, this imperative to bring outside realities inside bears repeating regardless of the current economic climate, because these kinds of changes and challenges will not stop.

All employees need to understand that the environment in which their employer operates has a direct impact on its ability to continue to employ them, pay them what they deserve, allow them to pursue self-improvement and personal career goals within the organization, and to make the capital investments that will help maintain productive, cost-effective operations. To do otherwise, to keep employees in the dark to guess and make assumptions, is dangerous on many levels. But at base, it isn't fair or honest. Have a conversation with your employees about these facts:

- Higher corporate taxes and increased energy costs mean less money to invest in people, plants and new equipment.

- These same costs also affect suppliers, which means the price of the goods and services we buy from them might increase, too.

- Higher taxes and energy costs also impede our customers' ability to buy our products.

- More regulations mean a further shifting of resources away from productive investments in people, plants and new equipment toward filling out forms, tracking data that has little to do with making the business run better, and dealing with government inspectors and agents.

- Higher healthcare costs will likely necessitate some reduction of benefits and/or increased co-pays.

- Raising prices is not always a viable option. We risk losing customers if our prices are too high. And we cannot grow and sustain our business if we lose customers.

- There is no deep, infinite well of money for salary and benefit increases, or for structural investments and capital improvements. It all comes from a business' ability to turn a profit on revenues *after expenses*. And if expenses go up, profits decline.

Don't misunderstand. I'm not arguing for a free-for-all business environment without regulation or taxes. But I am saying that these facts of life do impact businesses, and not always favorably.

I'm also saying that it's the responsibility of business leaders and managers of people to make sure employees appreciate the direct links between public policy decisions (i.e., to impose higher taxes and more regulations, etc.) by elected representatives and a business' ability to prosper, as well as the people that that business employs.

Social Media Behind the Firewall

Note: The following essay was adapted with a few changes from a two-part blog I posted in late 2011. So I find it remarkable that four years later the content is still relevant – which is to say that I'm not seeing as much movement toward internal social media as I had expected. To be sure, the large multinational companies are moving forward. But smaller firms, who stand to gain just as much benefit, are still balking and taking baby steps towards adopting even the simplest internal social media platforms. And I'm discovering that the same reasons cited here seem to be holding them back.

In recent years, something has been bubbling up in the world of employee communications. While some corporate communications managers weren't noticing, a growing proportion of their internal audience was bringing revolutionary new communications habits to the job.

This younger contingent, most of whom were born in the 1980s and later, has never known a world without cell phones, computers and the Internet. From their early years through college graduation, their primary means of connecting with friends has been electronically, through texting, instant messaging (IM), Facebook, Twitter, and online role-playing games (RPG).

Upon graduating college, many entered the business world. But their companies were communicating to them with blast emails and webcasts – i.e., those that were "modern" and "up-to-date." Some distributed memos on paper and printed newsletters.

153

The internal company website, if there was one, just sat there statically, with occasional news updates about the company. Maybe there was a blog, without an interactive feature, that hadn't been updated for several months. How passé. How very boring. How inefficient.

Fortunately, some organizations have addressed this shortcoming, dipping their toes in the water of internal social media. Yes, it's a scary concept, particularly to legal departments and some IT folks. I attended a peer conference of employee communications managers in late 2011 where "social media behind the firewall" emerged as the hot topic of the morning's discussion, even though it hadn't been on the agenda. Of the dozen or so companies represented at the table, only about half had initiated internal social media to some degree. But none had yet gone whole hog. One company had opened a chat function on its internal network, but made it available only to a fraction of its employees as a test.

In each case, the slow, deliberate pace of rolling it out was a means of proving its value and safety to skeptical legal and IT departments, as well as to work out the bugs and learn what does and doesn't work. The employee communications managers were pleased with the experiment and eager to let it grow.

So, what exactly is social media behind the firewall and why should communicators be interested? Social media has transformed the Internet into a place where people meet, learn, act, and react in real time. The kinds of activities that take place on conventional social media – Facebook, Linked In, Twitter, etc. – are essentially people meeting one another, introducing friends to other friends, and exchanging news, information and ideas electronically.

But aren't those the same kinds of activities that occur naturally within an organization over phone lines, in conference rooms, or spontaneously at water coolers, and in break rooms? Yes, but there is widespread resistance to bringing that capability electronically into organizations, even if it does mean improved communications for multi-site organizations. The primary barriers, I've seen, are IT and legal departments that fear hackers, or the spreading of confidential information externally.

I'm no techie, but from what I've learned at social media conferences and read in various sources, embedding social media on a company's own in-house server, behind the firewall, assures the security that companies need. Numerous vendors provide secure software, including IBM, which offers "Connections" – a suite of products to build internal social media. So, assuming we've cleared that security hurdle, what kinds of social media should we use internally? The answer depends on a company's culture, its size, the nature of its business, the number of employees, the number of locations, and the diversity of its internal audience.

Let's remember at the outset, however, social media is just another communications tool and should never be seen as a substitute for the real communicating that must occur in an organization between leaders, managers and employees: personal, face-to-face exchanges of information, ideas and insights.

To generalize, the selected social media tools should satisfy one core objective: to enhance and facilitate communications among and between employees, managers and leadership. In that light, consider three ideas:

- A *Linked In* style platform for multi-site companies would enable people to connect across departmental and national boundaries to discovery one another and their respective capabilities and talents. Individuals can readily find people of similar backgrounds and areas of specialty, and participate in relevant discussion boards where those in similar fields can discuss common challenges.

- A *Twitter*-like application might provide a venue where employees could post rapid-fire comments on everyday issues, as well as provide links to helpful and relevant internal and external websites. Managers and leaders could use it for quick communication of important, timely messages. At the same time, it would be advantageous for employees to "follow" company leadership, as well as their operational or functional management – in addition to their fellow team members – to stay abreast of important developments. Managers and leaders could use the platform to recognize outstanding work by individuals and teams, while peers could do the same, thanking individuals for their contributions to a given project, and the like.

- An internal *Facebook* type app would allow cohorts to stay abreast of one another's doings, particularly as it relates to working toward the company's strategies and objectives. Again, leaders and managers could use the app to spotlight important news, both inside and outside the company. (Available platforms like Yammer and Jive provide a hybrid of Twitter and Facebook type of opportunity for internal use.)

Meanwhile, leadership can eavesdrop on and/or participate in the discussions at will across any or all of such platforms, from wherever they are, whenever it's convenient.

Social media, then, can help leaders fulfill an important component of their jobs: staying abreast of what's going on within their organizations – the "listening" part of their jobs. But they can also participate by contributing to the conversation, trying out new ideas and the like, and correcting misinformation that may arise in conversation threads.

Let's assume your company lacks these channels. What are the challenges you're likely to encounter as you launch your own social media behind the firewall?

Certainly, as noted, the legal and IT departments might have confidentiality and security concerns. Is there any danger of employees sharing information that should not escape the confines of the company? Again, I'm not a tech guy but I've been reassured by friends who are that software, firewall protections, and passwords provide the necessary security today. Additionally, the enforcement of organization-wide non-disclosure agreements (NDAs) or their implementation for organizations that lack them through social media participants' online agreement should satisfy legal concerns.

So assuming you've solved the security issue, the biggest and most difficult barrier to overcome in launching an effective social media system is the same barrier that stymies most other corporate initiatives: *time* – i.e., no one has enough of it. Dozens of daily emails and countless meetings, to say nothing of the time needed to do their jobs, already overwhelm people. Who has the time or desire to monitor social media? Who has the time to build a profile page for a Linked In type platform? The answer lies principally in getting people to use it – admittedly a rather Catch-22 situation.

The more a person uses such platforms, the more comfortable they get with it, and the more they realize that it improves their awareness and understanding of the business while improving their effectiveness and adding to their own worth to the organization.

And, as more people use these platforms to an increasing degree, it reaches a tipping point where no one wants to be left out, and it becomes as natural as everyday conversation.

Ironically, these platforms have been shown actually to help people use their time more effectively. For instance, rather than dealing with dozens of daily emails, many people find that widespread use of internal social media significantly reduces the volume of internal email they have to handle.

To build participation, to reach that tipping point, leadership and managers must set the example. If it's important to leadership, it becomes important. Because of that alone, people will investigate at first, and then start using it, becoming regular participants.

A few years ago, Computerworld.com profiled three early adopters of internal social media. Deloitte, for instance, found that early adoption was slow. The company started with only a portion of the organization. Patricia Romeo, who led the effort, said, "People aren't going to go in as readily when the well is 75% empty. But with the encouragement of leadership, more people got involved and were soon demanding access to the rest of the organization."

Romeo advises continuing to build leadership support, even after the early-stage buy-in. "Make sure support is there throughout the organization," she said. Once the platform begins filling with valuable content, "it's really about viral adoption."

I would add that leadership support must be in the form of setting the example – i.e., using it themselves by becoming active participants while resisting their natural urge to fall back on their old communications vehicles – e.g., broadcast emails.

As to the second point, it's likely that nearly everyone in your organization already has a Linked In profile. Rather than ask them to replicate their profiles, make it easy by using Linked In's API to transfer profile data.

Any new means of communicating, for many in the organization, will represent change. And for most people, change is threatening. Don't burn the boats. Rather, maintain the established, conventional lines of communications. As younger employees build traffic on the internal social media network, their more senior peers will come to realize that a lot of business is being conducted there without them, and will soon join in – out of necessity.

Keep in mind that resistance may be greatest among older employees unaccustomed to social media, still more comfortable with their familiar modes of communication. As noted earlier, if the senior managers and the company leadership are actively engaged, they will have to get involved out of fear of being left behind, or perceived as out of the loop, or seen as old and fusty.

IBM, another company profiled in the Computerworld piece, was one of the first major companies to bring social media behind the firewall. Jeff Schick, VP of social software, said that poor adoption is rarely due to users who don't know how. Rather, it's because they didn't see the "why." Help them answer that question. To that end, the Computerworld article included a sidebar that's worth excerpting here. According to Amy Shuen, author of *"Web 2.0: A Strategy Guide,"* employees tend to have at least one of four goals when they use social networks.

1. *Quick access to knowledge, know-how and "know-who."* In their profiles, people can list skills, expertise and experience, as well as previous employers and people they know. As with Linked In, this helps simplify the job of locating people with the knowledge they need. This is particularly useful inside multidivisional, multi-site, and multinational organizations.

2. *Expansion of social connections and broadening of affiliations.* This is the Facebook model, in which the goal is to get to know people

better online by interacting with them and keeping up with their personal information.

3. *Self-branding and expression of a personal digital identity and reputation.* Before long, people get creative with their profiles and begin to think about how they want to be known in the company.

4. *Referrals/testimonials/benchmarking/RSS updating.* On social networks, the viral distribution of knowledge becomes important. People want to know how many of their "friends" have recommended a video or have joined a community and, in turn, if they discover something cool they want to spread the word.

Just bear in mind what I wrote before: that social media behind the firewall, at the end of the day, is just another communication medium. Don't confuse the tool with the task, which in this case is communications: the interaction between people and their exchange of information, ideas and insights.

If social media helps people become more effective communicators, then it may be something you want to consider for your own organization. But don't fall into the trap of adopting social media because it's the latest trend. And don't do it merely to expand your portfolio of communications tools. Do it because it makes sense, satisfies your organization's communication needs, and adds value.

What are we measuring?

To grow and to sustain themselves, companies make investments of money, time, and manpower into product development, research, marketing, infrastructure and expansion, and the many other components of operating a business. But boards of directors, investors, and shareholders want to know whether those expenditures are worthwhile, whether they truly bring value and growth to the company – i.e., "What's the return on investment?"

No component of the business today escapes ROI analysis. To answer that critical question across the many facets of the business requires some sort of measurement to gauge whether the money, time and manpower expended on something is yielding the intended results, perhaps even exceeding them. The more accurate, timely, and reliable the measure, the better.

Understandably, then, executives and managers are increasingly focused on measurement in its various forms through any number of means. The growing sophistication and availability of digital analytical tools is making measurement more readily attainable on an increasingly regular basis for an expanding list of activities – particularly because many of those activities occur in a digital environment, whether it's supply chain or sales data, external web traffic, or internal communications that occur on companies' intranet and/or internal social media.

In the context of the need to manage change, though, measurement is especially valuable to assure ongoing, smooth operations. Measuring the internal dialogue is especially valuable, when you consider that change initiatives and evolving strategies require understanding and buy-in from employees at all levels. We want to know: Are internal communications effectively driving the necessary behavior and attitude changes among employees? Digital measurement – internal analytics – can help us answer that kind of critical, time-sensitive question.

But in the rush to quantify anything and everything, our expectation is that those measurements will be monitored constantly. Yet monitoring is more than just logging numbers and percentage changes, looking for increases in understanding, say, over the course of time. We must also gain insights from them; insights that help us make adjustments in our decision-making, as well as what and how we communicate going forward.

For marketing departments, for instance, weekly fractional changes in market share up or down can mean millions of dollars, plus or minus. Determining the effectiveness of an expensive promotional campaign is built on the reactions of focus groups and measures of message penetration. So timeliness of those measures is a top priority once the product is in the marketplace to determine whether the promotional effort is "moving the needle."

But when we start measuring what happens among the people inside the organization, what are we really chasing? Let's assume we can get a regular read on what the employees are looking at on the internal website, how many are viewing what, for how long, what they're doing with it, and who they're sharing what with. Also, we can discern what they're chatting about on internal social media, and whether the chatter is positive, negative or neutral.

But what do we do with that information? Do we become obsessive about it? Do we become reactive? Do we become too reactive? Monitoring employee communications is certainly a critical and potentially valuable capability, insofar as it enables us to respond to employee information needs and adjust what we provide them, when, and through what channels. Beyond that, what are we looking for?

The problem with such internal monitoring is its potential to distract us from our core mission, to entice us to get ahead of ourselves – ahead of a curve that may or may not be critical, a curve that we may or may not be able to define – to make us too smart by half when what we really need to be providing to our internal audiences is something far simpler than what analytics might lead us to believe.

Let's remember our mission: At base, employees are just trying to do their job, to be good at it, to get better, to be acknowledged for their contributions, and to be aware of and understand the relentless changes that they and their company must adapt to.

As communicators, our primary role then must be to provide the context and relevant information to help employees stay abreast of the shifting marketplace and its multiple impacts on them and the company. If we do our jobs well – everything else being equal – then the company will thrive, employee attrition will stay low, and high quality talent will be attracted to our organization.

In the alternative case, the business will fumble its opportunities, under-estimates challenges, and fail to meet revenue and profit targets. The best talent will leave and the mediocre will remain. Growth and success will elude the organization.

In the short-term, measuring the quality of our employee communications, then, becomes an opportunity to stay on top of and eliminate the gaps in understanding among the internal audience that can fester and result in poor performance. And, it enables us to identify those communications activities that don't add value or understanding. Monitoring the conversation inside the organization, then, should be less about numbers and percentages and more about the content and context of that conversation.

If our analytics and monitoring allows us to determine whether key messages are resonating or not, whether people "get it" and are promulgating them in their conversations inside the organization, then the monitoring becomes truly valuable. It then is giving us critical and timely guidance to help us adjust our content, relevance, cadence and context to assure maximum effectiveness.

So in that regard, yes, measurement is important and can be valuable. But rather than becoming obsessed with upticks of tenths of percentage points of intranet traffic, we must focus instead on delivering timely, relevant information and context. If our measurement helps us do that, then it's doing its job. In that way, we are contributing to the success of the organization and its people, delivering meaningful returns on investment.

Communications as a Competitive Advantage

All economic recessions eventually come to an end. And when they do, corporate revenues, profitability and stock prices generally rise, while the Gross Domestic Product increases. Unemployment rolls decrease and hiring resumes. And when that happens, employees' behavior changes.

Specifically, the behavior to which I'm alluding concerns those latent desires to roam, to find a new job. Put another way, just because employee attrition rates are low during a recession doesn't mean that everyone is content and wants to stay put. It has a lot more to do with high unemployment rates and the dearth of available jobs than it does happiness and satisfaction on the job.

For the time being, for the sake of job security and a steady paycheck, people tamp down their latent desire to leave and find a new job, often putting up with otherwise untenable situations. But when the economy improves enough to resume its usual competition for talent, they will likely be on the prowl and jump at the first promising opportunity that comes along.

By the way, the first ones to leave will probably be among companies' best, most valuable people.

Regardless of the state of the economy, employee turnover is an expensive proposition on at least two levels. The monetary costs associated with finding, hiring, paying, training and retaining people are not insignificant. Organizations that experience high attrition rates are wasting a lot of invested capital, an investment that will have to be made all over again to replace the lost personnel. In other words, at companies with a high turnover rate, hiring costs are at least double what they need to be.

Secondly, and perhaps more important, retaining and building on the institutional memory and knowledge of your most valuable people is a reward that keeps on giving. So, being adept at hanging onto your best people is a distinct competitive advantage, more so when recessionary periods conclude.

Money that would have to be spent replacing lost employees is put to better use – such as on raises and bonuses to incentivize your best people, thereby creating a cycle that repeats itself.

But why do some companies experience high employee turnover while others don't, particularly in that critical transitional period coming out of a bad economy? Answer: Probably because of the quality of their internal communications.

Effective, ongoing employee communications, engagement and transparency are critical means to help prevent this loss of talent. The best managers and corporate leaders are skilled communicators, engaging their employees regularly, providing them timely and relevant information about the state of the company, while demonstrating their appreciation of their people. They listen closely and learn from their employees.

PepsiCo CEO Indra Nooyi used to characterize her attitude toward its employees with one word: "Cherish." In her annual letter to stockholders a few years ago, she wrote that it's one of her personal performance goals: "...cherishing our employees, what we call talent sustainability."

Being appreciated, having their views and insights heard and responded to is something that people treasure. They pay attention to supervisors, managers and leaders who communicate consistently and honestly. A symbiotic relationship is established: when people are listened to, they in turn listen closely; and when they are provided timely, relevant information, they in turn provide information necessary to the effective functioning of the larger organization.

Communication inside a company is its oxygen. Stifle people, put them in a box and restrict or inhibit the two-way flow of information, and they whither. Conversely, they thrive in a communication-rich environment.

Employees who are flourishing within an organization are engaged: engaged in its vision and the specific strategies that will help attain it. Engaged employees are more likely to stick around when the economy improves. Why would they want to leave a company that treats them with the respect and dignity they rightly deserve?

Invest in the future success of your organization by investing in employee communications and engagement now, and you will reap untold dividends for years to come.

How Mustaches are Like Social Media

Imagine you inadvertently overhear a snippet of your wife's conversation with a friend. Your wife says she doesn't like your new mustache, but hasn't said anything to you about it yet because she doesn't want to hurt your feelings. Nevertheless, she's eager for you to get tired of "that damned thing" and shave it off.

You've discovered a painful little truth. You're "just trying it out" and you think it looks pretty good. But you've gained a new insight into your wife's tastes. You'll probably shave it tomorrow morning.

Imagine, too, that you're the founder and president of a thriving and growing business. You've always assumed that your employees admire you and, for the most part, heed your counsel about how things ought to be done to assure continued growth and success.

Recently, your communications team installed a new social media app on the company's internal network that enables employees to meet and share ideas instantly, regardless of their location or time zone. It's an immediate hit. Employees are buzzing in the online chat room.

The head of communications suggests you spend a little time getting familiar with it and asks you to contribute to the conversation. You're busy and this new communications tool seems a bit frivolous. One evening at home, you have nothing else to do so you check it out. Amid the back-and-forth chatter about challenges and opportunities, customers, products, and competitors, however, you discover a few comments about you and your leadership team. Employees are wisecracking about your management style, your directives, your ideas, and even your habit of using certain catchphrases "all the time."

Now you're angry. The next morning, loaded for bear, you call in your communications VP to talk about it. He advises you to calm down and consider the comments as constructive criticism. You know he's right. So you think of them in the same way you do your wife's feelings about your mustache. You've discovered a difficult truth you weren't previously aware of.

It's a learning experience. The best organizations, after all, are learning organizations. And what this new social media experiment is doing, you realize, is allowing people to interact, share big and little ideas, and to learn together through means that previously did not exist.

People are having virtual conversations about topics that make the business better. Maybe their stray criticisms of your style are justified. Maybe you are a little stodgy in how you see things and how you operate. So your eyes are opened now.

Social media that is beginning to happen inside organizations follows on the heels of what has been going on outside for some time now. It just now is beginning to catch up. And there are important lessons that communicators can learn by studying what is happening in the outside world of marketing.

After all, what is employee communications if not internal marketing? Like conventional marketing, we must understand the various nuances of our target audience, which in our case lives within the confines of our organization. But this audience is not and never should be perceived as a monolith. Like external audiences of customers and potential customers, our employee audience has its idiosyncrasies.

As communicators, it's our responsibility, like marketers, to sort those out. We must fully understand what motivates our internal audience before undertaking the effort to convey important information to them with an eye toward affecting their behaviors – again, following the marketing model.

Marketers use social media to get ahead of the curve on product development, customer service, and customer satisfaction – all toward improving their customer relationships. They tap the external conversation to learn about the reception their new products are getting and to mine for new ideas, both for existing and new products. It's a newfound marketing goldmine.

But more to the point, the truly savvy marketers are using social media to build trust and brand loyalty with their customers by becoming effective peers – providing the right information at the right place at the right time for the right people.

Companies with a heavy quotient of customer interface like airlines and consumer product companies have learned how to leverage social media like Facebook and Twitter to get ahead of problems, and to address issues that may be troubling their customers. These and related actions build trust and improve brand loyalty.

Practitioners of employee communications know that these experiences can be applied to the relationships within an organization among its managers, leaders, and employees. They can effectively and positively impact the communication that sustains those relationships. We can use the internal social media tools we have at our disposal to do it: Yammer, Jive, intranet bulletin boards, blogs, or whatever works in your company.

While stimulating and increasing productive internal dialogue – regardless of managers' and employees' physical location – these tools also give leaders the opportunity to listen in on and contribute to the internal discussion, a productive, relevant conversation that was heretofore very difficult if not altogether impossible. Imagine the unlocked potential, especially in the context of being an effective peer.

The best managers and leaders are those that operate in the manner of a peer, speaking to employees as equals. They understand that their chief role is to help employees acquire the knowledge and necessary resources to do their jobs – and then get out of the way and let them do it.

What better way to uncover those needs, while cultivating trust and those critical internal relationships, than to engage in a robust, ongoing dialogue? And when the use of social media tools means that the dialogue can occur whenever and wherever you want inside the organization, then the possibilities for success and greatness are limitless.

Email in the Age of Social Media

In an era when people increasingly communicate via texts, IMs, Facebook posts and Tweets, email can seem antiquated. Yet within a corporate environment, email remains the best means of communicating quickly, efficiently, accurately, and reliably to individuals, selective groups of people, or the entire organization.

But it's imperfect – which, because it has become such an integral internal communications tool, is unacceptable. The most consistent complaints I hear about internal corporate email is that it is over-used, misused and abused; that there is an over-reliance on it as a medium when other means might be more effective; and that the sheer volume of email overwhelms most people.

The fact is most organizations haven't taken a consistent approach to email to assure that internal emails are achieving maximum efficiency. You may be old enough to remember a time when email communications were rare, or even non-existent. But they are so integral to today's business dynamic, it's easy to forget just how relatively young the medium is.

Perhaps as a consequence, email communications often exhibit more laziness, sloppiness and inconsistency than any other form of business communication. Poorly conceived emails can derail or even doom relationships, strategy implementation and general morale within organizations.

Are we as mindful of our email communications as we are of

our other written and oral communications? In other words, do we prepare our emails with as much care and thought as we do our oral presentations and written reports?

An equally critical problem is people getting deluged with emails. The result is often that much of it goes unread because people just don't have the time to look at everything. I've heard repeatedly that people get so many emails from their managers and company leadership that they're never sure which are important enough to merit their reading the entire communication.

Reminiscent of the boy who cried wolf, too many "important" and "urgent" emails from the CEO result in none being perceived as such. We are inclined to believe that any communication impacting the entire organization should come from the CEO (or president), since her/his responsibilities cross all profit centers, business areas, functions, and sites. But that would imply that his/her name go atop a significant number of communications – everything from an annual United Way appeal to the rollout of new product offerings and strategies. Pretty soon, everyone is getting a weekly email from the CEO.

In the interests of making better use of intra-company email, I'd like to suggest the following rules and guidelines both for the organization and for individuals.

Is it too important to use email? Email is so common in today's corporate environments that there is little to distinguish between critically important information and superfluous or basic information. If it's truly important, consider other methods besides email, including group meetings, face-to-face chats, videoconferences, or whatever other means work best in your organization.

From the top. To assure 100 percent readership of the communications from senior leadership that are *truly important*, adopt a clear delineation of the kinds of emails that should come from the top. As a general rule, matters involving the state of the business (e.g., quarterly and annual reports) and significant news on the progress of a new corporate strategy or initiative justify the CEO as the source. In some cases, however, where it impacts the entire organization, having it come from the leadership team as an impersonal entity makes more sense. And, instead of writing a tome, keep CEO communiqués as brief as possible. Provide a link to intranet pages or external sites for additional relevant information.

Broadcast? The number of broadcast emails to an entire organization should be limited. I often hear that people receive too many such emails and that, as a consequence, they deem them irrelevant – for instance, news of awards and rewards/recognition for individuals, or promotions of people within the company. In the end, you'll need an arbiter. Corporate Communications should be the clearinghouse for all such communications, making the determination whether a particular email is truly of interest and value to the entire organization, or just a segment. When in doubt, err on the side of fewer such communiqués and/or a smaller audience. Better still, these kinds of communications should be shifted onto the company intranet web sites for passive viewing.

ALL CAPS? Are you guilty of TYPING IN ALL CAPS? Or do you type everything in lower case, even when referring to people by name? This is no more acceptable than it would be in a printed document. Follow the same rules. Otherwise, you run the risk of coming across as disrespectful or sloppy.

Yes indeed, spelling and grammar count. Grammar, spelling errors and typos in emails are as inexcusable as they are in any other business document. Spell check is imperfect. Has your spell check ever allowed "now" when you meant "not?" There's a big difference.

After using spell check, proofread what you have written and make sure it's what you intend to say. For very important emails, print your draft and proofread that, too.

To bcc or not to bcc. Rather than listing dozens of recipients in the "To" or "cc" fields – some of whom might not appreciate having their email addresses shared so broadly – include these addresses in the "bcc" field instead. Obviously, it's a different story if everyone is from the same organization and expects to be copied on an email. Use your judgment.

Don't fight fire with fire. Have you ever gotten a nasty email from someone? The temptation might be to respond quickly in kind. The problems with that are two-fold. One, a hasty response might not be a fully considered one. Equally important, however, is that because some people are poor communicators by email, they might not even be angry. Better to use tact. If in doubt, give the person a phone call or visit them face-to-face to seek clarity.

Bad news. A major faux pas is delivering bad news by email, which can come across as cowardly, callous, or inappropriate. Believe it or not, I've actually heard of cases where people got laid off via email. When you have truly bad news or an emergency, either call the person(s) on the phone or, better still, talk to them face-to-face.

Be wary of the "thank-you" chain. In the context of a widely distributed email, if it merits a thank-you or congratulations type response, send it only to the original sender, not to the entire distribution list. Few things are as irksome than being cc'd on dozens of follow-up emails that say simply "thank you," "nicely done," or "congratulations."

Follow these basic rules and the value of your company's internal emails will rise appreciably.

Making the Most of Teleconference Calls

For most of my career, I've worked remotely. That is to say, I have had a home office for the past 20-plus years and worked there for established agencies, as well as operating as an independent consultant. When friends hear about my set-up, they often express envy about the short commute, but always add something along the lines of, "I couldn't do that. I wouldn't have the discipline."

In fact, my greatest challenge consistently has been associated not with self-discipline but rather with telephone technology, in particular, teleconference calls: not the content of the calls, but the general lack of protocol in most teleconference calls.

In early 2014, the *Wall Street Journal* reported in an article about this topic that time spent in conference calls in the U.S. is "expected to grow 9.6% a year through 2017, according to Wainhouse Research, a Boston market-research firm ... About 65% of all conferencing is still done by audio calls."

In that the expanding global economy continues to ensure that employees and outside contractors will increasingly be operating off-site, often at considerable distance from headquarters, the need for better teleconference technology and, especially, protocols for its use are imperative.

So it's safe to assume that we will have to continue to contend with unintelligible voices, people in the conference room who speak too loudly or not loudly enough, and other sins of teleconference calls, etc. That being the case then, let's establish some ground rules to minimize the challenges and make the best of a less-than-perfect technology.

- First of all, we shouldn't think of teleconference calls as "just another meeting." When there are several people in a conference room and one or more people tied in via the speakerphone, it should be treated as a different kind of meeting versus a purely face-to-face meeting.

- All participants should approach teleconference calls with good manners, exhibiting the utmost patience with and consideration of others, especially the people who dial in remotely. That means staying on topic, not engaging in side conversations, and not interrupting others.

- Establish an agenda beforehand with a clear and explicit purpose, and desired outcomes. Distribute the agenda before the meeting.

- Also before the meeting, provide a list of attendees and their roles, spelling out who will be in the conference room and who will be dialing in remotely. If possible, limit the number of participants to no more than eight or nine (including those on the phone). More than that and it tends to get chaotic.

- Be sensitive when one or more of the remote participants don't know all the people in the room. When we are all accustomed to working together in an office space, we are used to people's voices and their unique vocal mannerisms. Outsiders and newcomers dialing in are not. So it's imperative that people identify themselves each time they speak.

- Start the meeting with introductions, including name, role, and reason for participating in the meeting (if it's not obvious). Participants who don't know each other should introduce themselves, explain their roles in the project at hand and briefly explain what they hope to get out of the meeting. When latecomers enter the room, they should similarly introduce themselves. People dialing in late should announce themselves.

- Appoint a moderator. If the group leader is dialing in remotely, the moderator should be someone in the conference room. The moderator is responsible for maintaining order, staying on topic, and discouraging side conversations. The moderator should also make sure that remote participants get a chance to offer their two cents to the discussion.

- Like any meeting, there should be a note-taker.

- People in the conference room who wish to speak should be recognized, by name, by the moderator. They should move closer to and speak directly into the microphone.

- Remote participants should keep their phones on mute until they speak. Too often, ambient noises like a barking dog come blasting into the conference room speaker.

- If your phone line has elevator music for the hold function or you don't know, then don't put your phone on hold.

- The moderator should notice when remote participants are silent for too much of the meeting and actively seek their opinions and insights on the topic being discussed. The switch on the speakerphone tends to favor the voices and ambient noise in the room over those that are remote. The moderator should assume that silent remote participants have been unable to cut in.

- If someone in the room says or does something funny and everyone laughs, the moderator should let the remote participants in on the joke, repeating it if necessary.

- Meeting participants in the room should be sensitive to the absence of nonverbal cues such as facial expressions for remote participants. If necessary, the speaker or the moderator should help remote participants follow along by indicating that a comment was delivered with a grin or a frown, for instance, thereby helping them gain better contextual meaning, such as intended irony.

- If someone in the room has to leave early, they should excuse themselves aloud so that those on the phone know that that person is no longer in the meeting. Similarly, if you're on the phone and have to leave early, say so before hanging up.

- As the meeting wraps up, the moderator should restate the conclusions and go-forward actions, along with assigned responsibilities and deadlines. He/she should also double-check to make sure that the phone participants agree with his/her conclusions. If a follow-up meeting is necessary, take advantage of participants' presence and set up the next meeting.

- Before closing, the moderator should invite any final comments from the remote participants.

- The note-taker should type up and distribute the notes as soon as possible after the meeting, inviting participants to amend them as deemed necessary.

Bottom line: teleconference calls, like all meetings, should be seen as significant investments of people's time and energy. Treat them as such by ensuring the full participation of all attendees, including those dialing in remotely. Getting into the habit of following these simple rules will help ensure that teleconference calls are well worth the investment.

V. Customer Focus

V. Customer Focus

*"You've got to start with the customer experience and work back
toward the technology – not the other way around."*

Steve Jobs

Putting Clients Where They Belong: Front and Center

From its founding, any business' *raison d'être* is to provide customers with a product and/or service that improves their lives in some way. When a business consistently does that well, it succeeds and thrives – as well it should. Conversely, when a business loses that impetus, when its focus shifts away from its customers' needs and, instead, concentrates on the money it makes and a desire to make more, its demise is inevitable.

Such appeared to be the case with Goldman Sachs. In mid-March 2012, the world of Wall Street (and beyond) was abuzz on the heels of a provocative *New York Times* Op-Ed piece by Greg Smith titled, "Why I am Leaving Goldman Sachs."

In it, this vice president, a twelve-year veteran of the firm, explained that the company he came to know and love was a culture that had "revolved around teamwork, integrity, a spirit of humility, and always doing right by our clients. The culture was the secret sauce that made this place great and allowed us to earn our clients' trust for 143 years."

What had happened to Goldman Sachs, and why was this man so disillusioned that he had decided to leave? What had changed? According to Smith, "The firm changed the way it thought about leadership. Leadership used to be about ideas, setting an example and doing the right thing. Today, if you make enough money for the firm … you will be promoted into a position of influence."

As he wrote, "Today, many of these leaders display a Goldman Sachs culture quotient of exactly zero percent. I attend derivatives meetings where not one single minute is spent asking questions about how we can help clients. It's purely about how we can make the most money off of them."

Much the same story can likely be told of some of the big advertising, public relations, marketing and communications firms today. A lot of the effort they expend seems to be on expanding their service offerings to their clients, not necessarily because the clients need those extra services but because more service means higher retainer fees and greater agency profits.

The initial assignment, however small, is often used as a foot in the door to sell ever more services that the client may or may not need – like the proverbial door-to-door salesman. Some clients automatically push back, telling their agency to concentrate on delivering the promised service. And they're right to do so.

The correct way to grow an agency's business with a client is first to deliver the service for which it has been contracted. In fact, in addition to delivering on the promised services, surpass the client's expectations of the work, and it's likely the firm will be invited to provide additional services to address other challenges that the client is wrestling with. What's happened in this case is that the agency has earned the client's trust and respect.

Of course, it's a subtle dance because, in the course of working side-by-side in the client organization, other client challenges may become apparent to the outsider that the client may not see for being so close to it.

The agency is prepared and able to address these challenges, so it's a delicate case of offering the help. If the agency's honest motivation is to help the client deal with the problem rather than to "grow the business," there's a good chance it will be invited to do so – often without having to ask for it.

As Smith surely knows, a service-oriented business should bring to bear appropriate and necessary additional services to their clients, not principally for the supplementary revenue they might create but rather to provide those clients with complete solutions to their many challenges.

My experience has always been that when you provide great service to your clients, when you help them achieve or exceed the results they desire, they are more than happy to reward you with more opportunities, and they are pleased to know that you can make a profit, because you have made their lives better and likely made them look good within their own organization.

On the other hand, when clients are seen first and foremost as a source of revenue and profit rather than as a firm's core driver, the clients sense it. And frankly, such a firm's ultimate dismissal is predictable and justly deserved.

The larger question is whether the right or wrong attitude is embedded in the culture. When leaders of the firm talk within the agency of little else but revenue, profitability, cash flow, and their account teams' "billability," those on the lower rungs of the ladder correctly sense where the organization's priorities lie and, by extension, what gets rewarded.

These same principles apply in companies that provide manufactured products, where their customers expect reliability, consistency, and quality. Similarly, when managers in these companies focus more on the bottom line than on what delivers that, those organizations are also looking for trouble.

Smith understood these truths: "These days, the most common question I get from junior analysts about derivatives is,

'How much money did we make off the client?' It bothers me every time I hear it, because it is a clear reflection of what they are observing from their leaders about the way they should behave. Now project ten years into the future: You don't have to be a rocket scientist to figure out that the junior analyst ... doesn't exactly turn into a model citizen."

Smith didn't explicitly say so, but I believe that in ten years, some of those junior analysts will be vice presidents there, perpetuating its poisonous culture – that is, if Goldman Sachs is still in business.

And that's the question that emerges from this Op-Ed: will Goldman Sachs learn the wise and timely lesson that Mr. Smith offered them, change their ways, and survive? Frankly, it was a pretty simple warning: "I truly believe that this decline in the firm's moral fiber represents the single most serious threat to its long-run survival."

He added: "It astounds me how little senior management gets a basic truth: If clients don't trust you, they will eventually stop doing business with you."

So when a business loses touch with its culture, when its people cease following the guiding beacon that led the firm through nearly 150 years of success, what should it do to regain its footing? Smith advised that it should "... make the client the focal point of your business again. Without clients you will not make money. In fact, you will not exist... And get the culture right again, so people want to work here for the right reasons. People who care only about making money will not sustain this firm – or the trust of its clients – for very much longer."

Wise counsel – not just for Goldman Sachs but also for any business.

Employees are Central to the Customer Experience

In the days before mobile telephones, when AT&T was the monopoly providing landline telephone service, comedienne Lily Tomlin played a recurring comic role as "Ernestine," a telephone operator. After treating a caller rudely and hanging up, she would look at the audience, grin sourly, snort and say, "We're the phone company. We don't care. We don't have to."

To those of us on the receiving end, Ernestine was painfully real. It often felt like AT&T could and did operate any way it wished without fear of losing customers – there was no where else to go for telephones or phone service. Ernestine's sneering uncaring attitude was emblematic of how people experienced and perceived "Ma Bell."

How far we've come in our choices. The end of the AT&T monopoly, and the advent, technological advancements, and rapid growth of mobile telephony have marginalized conventional landline telephones. But more than just the landscape of the phone business has changed since the day of Ernestine. The drivers and predictors of business success also have changed.

In a brilliant and insightful book titled *Outside In*, Harley Manning and Kerry Bodine of Forrester Research made the case that today, the chief avenue to business success is the customer experience; i.e., "How your customers perceive their interactions with your company."

Even monopolies like the old Ma Bell couldn't get away with abusing customers and expect to stay in business today. Forget about thriving. The bar for excellence is constantly rising. All businesses must excel at the customer experience or risk the onset of a death spiral that will end in their demise.

Competition is not always just other companies providing the same products or services; it's often another company in an entirely different industry setting new standards for customer service, responsiveness and quality.

Assuring that people become loyal customers involves making it easy to find, buy and use your products/services. This is a complex exercise encompassing all components of and people within your organization. At its heart, the authors explain, the customer experience is what happens when your customers try to *learn about* your product/service offerings, *evaluate* them, *buy* them, *use* them and, if necessary, *get help* when they have a problem with them.

In the end, it's about how customers feel about those many different encounters. Are they happy, excited and reassured, or disappointed and frustrated? *Outside In* first defines the customer experience and describes its value before delving into the disciplines of superior customer experience and the paths that companies can take to assure that the customer experience becomes central to their business.

Look again at that list of the five components of the customer experience and you'll realize that, to some degree or other, they all involve employees. Though the book touches on the subject throughout, from my perspective, the ability of a company to engage its employees in the company's larger mission is central to its ongoing ability to deliver a superior experience for customers time and again throughout the experience cycle – thus ensuring their continued loyalty and positive word-of-mouth. In other words, every employee must be engaged in delivering that superior experience.

It's not just the customer-facing people – those in the retail stores or the people who provide tech service and sales support on the 800-number. It involves everyone, because every role in the company can make a difference. Even if you banished Ernestine and her kind from your company, that would not be enough to assure a superior experience for all customers.

I once heard the CEO of a client company speak at a company town meeting for the employees about the unacceptable level of customer defections they were experiencing. She said, *"These are things that we can control.* This isn't just about customer service. This isn't just about retail stores. This is everybody in the business understanding how each one of us impact this." And she was right.

We once helped a financial services company as it made a radical change in the way it went to market. Instead of focusing on products it created and sold as it always had, it shifted its focus to its largest customer segment – small business owners – and their unique needs. Internal changes were necessary and a relatively easy shift for the customer-facing employees. Not so everyone else.

The employees that developed, marketed and supported the new products and services had a tougher shift. So our communications strategy sought to engage all employees across the organization in the monumental change by helping them gain a better sense of the world in which customers bought and used its offerings.

The program required managers to involve their teams in detailed exercises – using actual video interviews with small business owners – to be better able to think like customers and fully appreciate the challenges they faced. The goal of the program was to help them make the connection between the products the company provided and how they could help customers surmount their challenges.

We knew the program succeeded when we learned that the IT department – about as far removed from direct customer interactions as any department – figured out how they could contribute to improving the total customer experience by overhauling the externally facing website to make it more responsive and user friendly. It made quite a difference, as many customers noted in follow-up surveys.

Few outside of IT would ever have identified that as an opportunity for improvement. No one in the executive suite would have seen how a fix to the website could thrill customers. No one else would have imagined that an internally focused operation could have such an impact on the external customer experience.

The point is, the entire organization must get in customers' shoes and think like them, and better appreciate their personal challenges and needs. That way, employees will do their job most effectively toward the company's larger mission of delivering a superior customer experience.

For additional insights and perspectives on this topic, see "Cultivate Your Employees' Extreme Trust," page 106.

Connecting to the Customer

The parameters that define the Employee Communications operation in a typical company, for the most part, are fairly restrictive: develop strategies while managing internal media to reach employees with timely and relevant messages that engage them in the business, its purpose, goals, and strategies.

And that's as it should be. But that definition leaves a lot of room for interpretation. Employee Communications operations should also ensure that the employees engage the customer to gain an accurate and timely understanding of their world.

In my first book, "Inside the Organization," I touched on this topic in an essay titled "Listen to the Customer's Voice" (page 72), I wrote how we had developed videos of customer interviews that were then shared across the organization to help all employees better appreciate critical customer needs and expectations.

The insights it contained are still true. In fact, they've become even more critical in the intervening years as companies increasingly recognize the central importance of delivering a customer experience that not only meets expectations but also elicits a *"Wow!"* from customers and helps build long-term loyalty.

To that end, I want to revisit the topic from a slightly different approach, because it is so central both to a company's ultimate success and to the role that employee communications can and should play in helping achieve that success: building greater employee awareness, understanding, appreciation, and empathy for the customer and the world in which the customer must operate and compete.

As noted several times in this section on "Customer Focus," the company's ability to deliver on its promises lies with its employees – not just the people who engage the customer one-on-one, but also those in the background, the ones supporting the customer-facing employees in any number of ways.

It stands to reason that every employee would do his/her job far better with a deeper understanding of the customer. Regardless of their role, they should have at least one opportunity to observe or participate directly in customer relations. Let me share two situations in which employee communications operations had a hand, in terms of designing, selling to senior management, and implementation.

One client was a component manufacturer selling into the OEM (original equipment manufacturer) market. The company would organize annual visits by all their new employees to a customer's assembly plant so they could see how their components were being used. The customers understood the benefit for these visits and were enthusiastic hosts, participating in planning the visitors' exposure to their operation. Not only were employees shown assembly lines where their components were added to the finished products. They also were given a tour of the ancillary operations that supported the plant, including:

- How the just-in-time supply chain system worked, and why timely delivery from suppliers was critical.
- How and why quality control checks were embedded throughout the process, and what those checks entailed, and why.
- The various roles and responsibilities of the people who worked on the assembly line.

- The packaging, and final quality check on the finished goods before they were loaded for distribution.

For the people directly involved in the fabrication and quality control of the components, as you would guess, these trips to customer plants were real eye-openers. While their managers had drilled into them the importance of total quality, they now saw with their own eyes why that was so critical to the ultimate value of the OEM's finished products and, in turn, their customers.

What about those without hands-on roles in the production process? Why did they go, and what did they get out of it? Quite simply, seeing how their company's products were used enabled people in all other parts of the business to connect their role and the importance of doing their job well to help deliver to the customer's expectations. Additionally, the pride that comes from actually seeing where and how the fruits of your organization's efforts are used is no small matter.

One other brief case... Another client made a highly specialized resin that provided one brand name paint's rust-resistance for use on a pickup truck trailer hitch. One of the lab chemists who helped refine the production process got the chance to visit the plant where the trucks were made. Their resin was sold to a paint manufacturer who in turn sold it to the component maker who produced the trailer hitch that went on the pickup.

The chemist spoke to the quality assurance manager who told him how critical it is that that trailer hitch never rusts. The chemist confidently assured him that it would not, and then went on to explain in layman's terms exactly why it wouldn't.

Talking about the experience months later, you could sense his pride in retelling the story. He had gone from being, in his mind, a simple lab chemist, removed from the world in which the fruits of his efforts were actually used, to being able to explain to the end user why and how his contribution was critical – as well as reliable.

In turn, the chemist came to understand how important his role was in meeting the expectations of the ultimate customer – the guy who bought the pickup and drove it for eight or ten years without worrying that the trailer hitch would rust and fall off.

One of the most difficult challenges any company faces is creating and maintaining awareness and insight into the customer experience among its entire employee population. To the extent that the company's employee communications professionals can help sustain and enhance that through efforts such as these could be one of its most valuable contributions to the perpetuation and success of that business.

Cultivate Positive Client Relationships

The full value of a consulting firm's services comes to fruition when it can establish functional, respectful relationships with the key people inside the client company, especially the person they work with regularly – the primary client liaison.

A meeting of minds must take place early in that client-consultancy relationship, and a level of respect for one another established that recognizes the value and talents that each brings to the relationship and how best to work together to maximize the benefit to the company. However, that kind of trusting relationship is virtually impossible when one side, without just cause, casts the other in a disparaging light.

"Bruce," an acquaintance of mine, told me about his former employer, a small public relations agency. As his story unfolded, I soon understood why he had left. His former boss, "Mike," president of the agency, was uniquely talented at scouting and landing new business. That was his gift, and he knew it, though he wasn't very skilled at dealing with the nitty-gritty of servicing those clients and fulfilling the promises of his sales pitches.

Fortunately, he was also conscious of that weakness and handed off that responsibility to others, including Bruce, who he put in charge of client service. As agency president, Mike had to maintain some client contact, especially early in the relationship, which meant leading the initial strategy meetings with the client liaison. And that's where the trouble often cropped up.

Bruce says that, over the course of his three years at this agency, he could not think of a single client liaison that Mike did not disparage – that is, once he was back in the office away from client ears. One was "incompetent." The next was "an idiot." Another was a "perfect example of the Peter Principle."

What bothered Bruce the most and what eventually drove him from the firm was the poisonous effect Mike's continuous bad-mouthing had on the general attitude toward its clients by the firm and its people. Bruce would hear a junior staffer mocking his client liaison using Mike's terminology, and would pull that junior person aside and patiently explain the downside of such attitudes.

Bruce had a couple of private chats with Mike, urging him to tone down the client criticisms, or at least to keep them to himself, because he was creating negative attitudes within the agency towards its clients. He reminded him that it was they who helped the firm meet its payroll and allowed them to make a profit.

The negativity would abate for a time, but would soon be seeping back into the general agency buzz. While it may be okay to disagree with a client contact's approach or her/his interpretation of the facts, it's not okay to disparage that person's intelligence or competence, regardless of how you may feel. It's best to keep those thoughts to one's self.

Sure, I've worked with clients where the chemistry wasn't right from the outset and the relationship never quite gelled. Consequently, we felt constrained, prevented from doing our best work.

Conversely, I have been in client relationships that I hated to see end, where the chemistry was fantastic and, together, the client and firm did superb work to the benefit of the client's company. I still count some of those people as good friends. And yes, there were those rare occasions (I can count three over the course of my twenty-five years in the business) where the client liaisons were indeed jerks; where they sabotaged our work at every turn or questioned every little thing we did; where they actively tried to make us look bad, for their own twisted reasons. And in those cases, I would have been in agreement with "Mike" in his negative assessments. Even still, I kept it to myself and worked hard.

Fortunately, those cases are rare. Why would Mike feel compelled to badmouth every client liaison? Bruce says he asked himself that question all the time, and even went so far as to ask it directly of Mike himself. There was no clear or obvious answer. Mike just brushed off the question. Perhaps it was deep-seated personal insecurities that led him to disparage clients. Whatever it was, it really didn't matter because the effect was the same.

How can we do our best work, get engaged in the client's challenges and opportunities, if our boss thinks the guy is an incompetent fool? We can't. He has poisoned the well and every sip we take thereafter is contaminated. We find ourselves privately second-guessing the client and her/his input and opinions, seeing them through Mike's tainted, negative lens, no matter how hard we try to look past it.

I'm not suggesting the opposite: rose-colored glasses, pretending everything is wonderful and the client is a genius or a saint. Instead, we must tamp down the negative attitude and strive to cultivate positive, mutually supportive working relationships. People do their best work in a constructive environment, one in which they feel engaged and connected to others on the team, particularly the client liaison. It behooves us all, both the outsiders and the inside liaisons, to do all we can to cultivate the relationship and to be positive in our quest for excellence on behalf of the client company.

Playing to Your Audience

Walter Isaacson's biography of Steve Jobs, published shortly after the CEO's untimely death in late 2011, was particularly striking to me in the tale of the development of the Apple Stores. The reason it caught my attention was how it cut to the core challenge of communications and marketing: the importance of really knowing your audience.

Ron Johnson oversaw the development and rollout of the ultimately very successful Apple Stores – and they indeed proved to be a *huge* retail success, by the way. Just to put it in perspective, consider the following citation from the book: "In July 2011, a decade after the first [stores] opened, there were 326 Apple Stores... The average annual revenue per store was $34 million, and the total sales in fiscal 2010 were $9.8 billion."

What intrigued me about this story within a biography was how Johnson revolutionized the stores' concept with a last-minute change in approach to the stores' layout, a brainstorm he had in the middle of the night shortly before the prototype was to be introduced to Apple's Board of Directors.

An archetype of the Apple Store was built in 2000 in a warehouse near the Apple campus in Cupertino. It was furnished completely, and then the design team hung out there, tweaking and adjusting it until they felt comfortable with the concept and its many components. Johnson led the effort for Apple, and Jobs would stop by about once a week to monitor progress and make suggestions for improvement. After fiddling with nearly every aspect of the prototype repeatedly, Jobs and Johnson felt they were ready to invite the Board to the warehouse to see it. But the day before the unveiling, Johnson awoke in the middle of the night with a bad feeling:

> *"…They had gotten something fundamentally wrong. They were organizing the store around each of Apple's main product lines… But Jobs had begun developing a new concept: the computer as a hub for all your digital activity. In other words, your computer might handle video and pictures from your cameras, and perhaps someday your music player and songs, or your books and magazines. Johnson's predawn brainstorm was that the stores should organize displays not just around the company's four lines of computers, but also around things that people might want to do."*

Confronting Steve Jobs with bad news was always dangerous, but Johnson felt strongly about it. On the way over to see the prototype, Johnson shared with him his misgivings and urged that they start the design process all over again. After exploding in anger, Jobs sat silently in the car and thought about what Johnson had recommended as they made their way to visit the model. Jobs then presented it to the design group with these words: "Ron thinks we've got it all wrong. He thinks it should be organized not around products but instead around what people do." [Long pause] "And you know, he's right… We've got only one chance to get it right."

And boy, did they get it right. Have you ever been to an Apple Store when it wasn't crowded? Me neither. While the other mall stores near it may be quiet, the Apple Store is noisy, swarming with customers and browsers – even on weekday mornings when the rest of the mall is quiet. It never ceases to amaze me.

This demonstrates a core principle of successful marketing

and, in the same sense, successful communications. Reach people on their turf; respond to how they live their lives and communicate, not how you want them to, and you're guaranteed to get their attention.

It is something I learned early in my career, a lesson that has never failed me. When I was a suburban beat reporter for a daily newspaper, once while struggling with a particularly complicated story about a town commission's meeting, I grew frustrated at finding the right narrative. Knowing that I was facing a fast-approaching deadline, my editor pulled me aside to help me get focused. He posed a series of questions that cut to the core of my dilemma. His questions weren't about the point of the story or its details, but rather about my readers.

Who were my readers? What was their likely interest in the story and the decisions of this particular commission? How would the commission's actions and decisions affect my readers? So, putting myself in their shoes, what did I think they would likely want to know? As the effect of his questions began to sink in, I fairly jumped out of my seat to return to my writing. The light bulb had gone on and I whipped out the story easily and quickly.

What I had been missing was a clear understanding of focus and purpose. Without either, writing is an exercise in a vacuum to no end. The same is true in corporate communications and marketing.

When you expend the necessary upfront effort to get to know and appreciate your audience, to understand what truly drives them and what they want and need from you, you are well past the halfway point in your journey to connect with them successfully. Will the result always be on par with the Apple Store? Maybe not, but you don't stand a prayer for success on any level without that crucial first step of inquiry. The germ of the idea about the customers' world that disturbed Ron Johnson's sleep on night made all the difference.

Two Tales of Customer Service

Depending on which company or industry we're talking about, a company's relationship with its customers has a range of realities. But being on the receiving end as a client always brings its meaning into sharp focus.

When your scheduled flight from point A to point B is delayed, and delayed again repeatedly so that your actual arrival is hours past the promised time and your luggage is lost in the ether, that airline's attitude toward you and other customers quickly becomes critically important to your mental state and well-being, to say nothing of your personal plans.

Ditto the computer software marketer that chooses to cease upgrading a favorite application you've been using and become dependent on after several years.

In fact, these two examples are based real experiences that I have had. First, United Airlines. Yes, I admit that on this particular occasion, my flights from San Diego to Houston and Houston to Boston were on time. The on-board service was adequate. This, I'm sorry to say, was the exception. It's not just true with United but also with the other legacy airlines with which I've done business: Delta and American (and US Airways).

I bring this up because, at the time, United was in the throes of combining operations with the newly acquired Continental Airlines. Though my flights that week were on Continental aircraft, staffed by crews wearing Continental uniforms, everything else about the experience was United. We were reminded of that repeatedly.

What got my attention, however, was the short on-board video greeting from United's CEO, Jeffery Smisek. The prime purpose of the welcome, it soon became apparent, was to apprise us of the progress the company was making in merging the two formerly independent airlines.

So what do you think was the first thing Smisek mentioned? That they were making good progress repainting their planes. Huh? Would new paint jobs improve on-time performance? He didn't say anything about merging their two distinctly different cultures, nor anything about how they were working to improve customer service resulting from combined operations. Nope. Just the paint job.

Furthermore, a message printed on the cocktail napkins that accompanied the beverage service said the following: "Planes change. Values don't. Your priorities will always be ours." Really? Is United telling us that their values parallel our priorities? Like on-time flights and no lost luggage? I doubt it.

Sorry for the cynicism but I've seen this movie before, especially in the airline industry. Can anyone tell me with a straight face that the Delta-Northwest merger improved service to the cities those two formerly independent carriers serve? Ask the same question as US Airways and American Airlines move forward combining their operations.

So let's be honest: the primary, sometimes the only purpose of airline mergers is to realize the cost savings that combined operations will yield. Period. It most assuredly is not because the execs sat down and said, "Let's merge so that we can improve service to our customers." If Mr. Smisek himself told me that to my face, I'd laugh and still wouldn't believe him. If that is, in fact, among their priorities, then it's toward the bottom of a very long list. Sorry, but I know these airlines too well. And I'm sure you do, too.

Here's a different case in point: different industry, different type of product, and different type of customers. Intuit is a software company, most famous for its Quicken brand of personal and business financial software.

I had been using Quicken on my Macintosh computers for at least 15 years – perhaps longer – when the situation changed abruptly. The software had helped me manage my finances quite well, for which I was grateful. But apparently, due to a corporate decision, that had to end.

I'm not entirely sure why, because I am not a software expert. But with the introduction of Mac OS X 10.7 (a.k.a. Lion) in mid-2011, Quicken no longer worked on Macintosh. I started digging into this because I was reluctant to give up this helpful software, and learned that Intuit had not updated Quicken in more than five years and, further, had no intention to update it so that it would operate on the new Mac OS X.

An exchange of fruitless emails ensued with their tech support people. Sifting through their extended namby-pamby answers, I surmised that they really didn't care about Macintosh customers anymore. They suggested that I load Windows on my Mac so that I can continue to use Quicken. Of course, that answer fails to acknowledge that to do so, I would have to acquire Windows and a Windows-compatible version of Quicken. Aside from the added cost, I didn't want the tech hassle.

So Intuit lost me (and no doubt countless other Mac users) as a customer. I found it hard to believe that Intuit would walk away from Mac users, a target audience that happens to be the fastest growing among all computer users.

That's their choice. My choice was to seek an alternative to Quicken.

What's the lesson here? It's not difficult to find the flip side of good customer service and the long-term value and good will it brings to the company willing to commit to it. Why am I exclusively a Macintosh user for 20-plus years? Why do I pay such close attention whenever Apple introduces a new product? Because Apple's tech support is second to none. They will not let you go until they are confident that they have solved your problem. Apple offers a myriad of ways to access customer service: over the phone, on-line discussions and FAQs, and their famous Apple Genius Bar where you can get face-to-face help on virtually any problem.

(Not coincidentally, Apple is thriving. Check their revenues, profits and stock price for proof.)

Compare that experience to the frustration felt standing at the end of a snaking line at the airport customer service counter after your United (or Delta, or US Airways, or American) flight has been canceled, or feeling abandoned by the software company that had provided you with a highly functional and helpful application.

Who's the real loser in these instances? Hint: it's not the customer.

About the Author

Jack LeMenager is an independent communications and change management consultant with more than twenty-five years of experience in the business, including assignments in internal communications and business-to-business marketing communications for some of the world's leading companies. His clients have included businesses in industries like consumer goods, insurance, aviation, automotive, medical devices and equipment, pharmaceuticals, chemicals, paper, professional services, and others.

He is the author of the companion book to this volume, "Inside the Organization: Perspectives on Employee Communications," a collection of fifty-four thematically organized essays on communications and human relationships inside and outside the business world (which has been revised and updated).

A California native (Santa Rosa), he earned his Bachelor of Arts degree in English at Willamette University (Salem, OR), including a year abroad studying at the University of London. He began his career as a newspaper reporter and editor in Connecticut.

He and his wife, Carolyn, reside in Winchester, MA.

He welcomes your thoughts, comments or questions on this book, as well as any related topics. Please feel free to drop an email at: j.lemenager@comcast.net.